Russell Kelso Carter

The Tree of Knowledge

A startling scientific study of the original sin, and the sin of the angels, with a history of spiritism in all ages

Russell Kelso Carter

The Tree of Knowledge
A startling scientific study of the original sin, and the sin of the angels, with a history of spiritism in all ages

ISBN/EAN: 9783337042202

Printed in Europe, USA, Canada, Australia, Japan

Cover: Foto ©Lupo / pixelio.de

More available books at **www.hansebooks.com**

THE
TREE OF KNOWLEDGE;

A Startling Scientific Study
Of the Original Sin, . . .
And the Sin of the Angels,

WITH A HISTORY OF

SPIRITISM IN ALL AGES.

By Captain R. Kelso Carter, C. E.,

AUTHOR OF

"*Alpha and Omega; or, The Birth and Death of the World.*"

SAN FRANCISCO, CAL.:
O. H. ELLIOTT, Publisher
1894.

CONTENTS.

	PAGE.
PREFACE	9

Part I. — Spiritism, Old and New.

CHAPTER I.
NEW SCIENCE AND OLD TRUTH . . . 19

CHAPTER II.
BRIEF HISTORY OF SPIRIT MANIFESTATIONS . . . 33

CHAPTER III.
SPIRITISM — ITS OUTER FRAUDS . . . 48

CHAPTER IV.
"TRANSCENDENTAL PHYSICS" . . . 80

CHAPTER V.
THE LATEST PHENOMENA . . . 119

CHAPTER VI
SPIRITISM — ITS INNER "MYSTERIES" . . . 135

Part II.—The Original Sin.

CHAPTER I.
THE SEX QUESTION . . . 185

CHAPTER II.
THE SIN OF THE ANGELS . . . 220

CHAPTER III.
THE FALL OF MAN . . . 278

CHAPTER IV.
WHAT IS THE "CARNAL MIND?" . . . 294

CHAPTER V.
THE CROSS AND PHALLIC WORSHIP . . . 337

CHAPTER VI.
THE MYSTERY OF INIQUITY . . . 378

CHAPTER VII.
THE CLIMAX . . . 402

LIST OF ILLUSTRATIONS.

PLATE.		PAGE.
1. "The Woman Wailing for Her Demon Lover"		Frontispiece
2. The Mighty Conflict		17
3. The Rally		25
4. Michael and Lucifer		35
5. The Last Defeat		41
6. The Spirit of Vile Fraud		49
7. The Genius of Fable		55
8. Foster Reading Folded Papers		61
9. The Blood Writing		65
10. The Famous Slate Writing		71
11. Spirit Photography		75
12. Heliodorus Punished in the Temple		85
13. Knots in Endless Cord		97
14. Table and Wooden Rings		107
15. Chains of Darkness		117
16. The Pit of Fire		127
17. The Messenger of Evil		137
18. Drawing Nearer		147
19. The Creation of Eve		157
20. Innocence		171
21. Envy of Others' Peace		187
22. Waiting His Opportunity		201
23. The Seduction		213

LIST OF ILLUSTRATIONS.

PLATE.		PAGE.
24.	THE FALL ACCOMPLISHED	225
25.	THE BIRTH OF FEAR	235
26.	THE FIRST SHAME	247
27.	THE SENSE OF GUILT	259
28.	DRIVEN OUT	271
29.	SIN BRINGING FORTH DEATH	281
30.	THE FALL OF SODOM	289
31.	THE STRONG MADE WEAK	301
32.	THE BLACK RIVER	309
33.	THE HOSTS OF THE LOST	319
34.	SERPENTS OF REMORSE	329
35.	MISERY IN COMPANIONSHIP	339
36.	THE POINT IN A CIRCLE	347
37.	VARIATIONS OF THE CROSS	353
38.	THE BREADTH OF REDEMPTION	371
39.	THE DEPTH OF REDEMPTION	391
40.	THE HEIGHT OF REDEMPTION	399
41.	THE HALLELUJAH CHORUS	419

The publisher acknowledges the use of plates 13 and **14 from Zollner's book,** "Transcendental Physics." The magnificent designs of **Gustave Doré are so** perfectly suited to the **argument of this book that** it hardly seems possible they could have been more appropriate if the great French artist had drawn them specially for this work. Many of the illustrations are from original designs, and were engraved expressly for this volume.

PREFACE.

This book may rightly be styled "unique." There is nothing like it in the world, although many things in it are to be found under the shadow of great and honored names, like those of Dr. A. J. Gordon, of Boston, and G. H. Pember, of England. When such men think there is something in the theories presented herein, ordinary minds may well examine the evidences without allowing prejudice to forestall judgment.

This book calmly examines the available statements and facts concerning the *real nature* of the sin committed by Eve, and of the sin of the wicked angels with the daughters of the antediluvians. It studies into the special sin of the seven nations of Canaan, and couples these with many startling facts of more modern history, and with the evidence of the existence and practice of similar evil in the present day, and with the predictions of Scripture that the same sin of the angels shall be reproduced in the present age just before the Crisis and the Coming Golden Age.

A brief history of Spiritualism in all ages is given, with a thorough explanation of its most important public "tests," including the latest and most extraordinary phenomena, while the veil is withdrawn from its so-called "mysteries."

Many will undoubtedly ask, "Why did you write such a terrible book?"

He who knows of a pitfall in the road, and fails to warn his neighbor, whom he sees traveling that way, is guilty if the neighbor tumbles in.

"But most people never heard of such deviltry; why then tell them of it?"

That is the old, old foolish reason given for trying to keep children ignorant of evil in the world. Many a man has gone astray because he did not know the first signs of the enemy's approach. The physician who gives warning of the coming of a dreadful plague, and who minutely describes its disgusting symptoms, is looked upon as a public benefactor, even if he cannot suggest a remedy. But if he can, at the same time, point out **a specific,** his monument is assured in the temple of fame.)

" But why do you use such plain language about **the most** delicate matters ? "

The scout who brings tidings **of the** approach of the enemy in general terms is worthy of praise, **and receives it.** (But the one **who** supplies his **commander with a** detailed plan of the camp **of the foe, the situation of** each piece of ordnance, **the number and** position of his reserves, the plan **of his** intended attack, and the time of **the** movement, deserves immortal honor. **It may** be well to inquire how one can uncover the very depths **of the** " bottomless pit " itself in order that others **may not** stumble into it unawares, and not use " plain language."

There is no time in this tremendous and crucial age **to** speak of " the gentleman in black " and of " hades." (The hurrying earth is rushing **towards** that quarter of the heavens from which some day **will** suddenly sweep down upon it the terrible meteoric storm that will bring the awful changes of the "Coming Crisis," and usher in the next Age with all its marvelous conditions, and the very air is thick with the rumors of the approaching cataclysm. (Some of you may one day thank God that I was moved to tell you about these things, when you find yourself thereby qualified to warn a loved one of the treacherous evil that is so attractively disguised.)

If you think the Bible deals in metaphors when it talks about not "wrestling with flesh and blood, but with wicked spirits in heavenly places," you will have to differ. God has declared that "In the last days perilous times shall come, and men shall give heed to *seducing spirits*." I am trying to reveal to you the character and plan of attack of these same "spirits." "Surely in vain the net is spread in the sight of any bird." The battle is on, and in view of its terrible nature and in the very face of such a foe, "a spade is a spade."

This book has been written at the earnest request of sober-minded men and women who attended my lectures upon this subject in the city of San Francisco, where I first delivered them. The only censure I received was for not speaking plainly enough, and I was urged to write out the whole thing so that the warning might go abroad. Hence this book. In order to fully grasp the scientific facts it is necessary to read my " Alpha and Omega, or the Birth and Death of the World."

☞ (Remember that I am not the author of the theory of an unnatural intercourse with the demon world. The Bible repeatedly makes the statements on this point, and scientific research presents a great deal of curious evidence. I merely examine the statements. If you will find fault, it must be with the Bible, but no man can truthfully say that these theories originated with

THE AUTHOR.

PART FIRST.

Spiritism—Old and New.

Plate 2.　　　THE MIGHTY CONFLICT.

CHAPTER 1.

New Science and Old Truth.

WE live in a strange day. It is an epoch in the world's history. The revolutions of time bring to the surface startling evolutions of human thought and belief. What was considered the truth yesterday is rejected as false to-day, and the foolishness of to-day becomes the acme of wisdom before the morrow's sun has set. About the best coat of arms for modern religio-scientific thought would be a kaleidoscope *rampant* on a field *d'or*. (He or she who can formulate the most striking innovations, in such a way as to accumulate the largest amount of gain, both for themselves and their disciples, has the quickest and most numerous following.

Now, no matter what skeptics may choose to say, one fact stares us in the face,—this is characteristically a religious age. Note, not necessarily a godly or Christian age, but a religious one. And who does not know that there are many religions in the world? Their name is legion. But there never was a time when the advancing tides of human progress, human discovery, and human invention made such daring and impetuous inroads upon the religious coasts of thought. The Athenian spirit is abroad again, to tell and hear some new thing; and, following the laws of supply and demand, so potent in mortal affairs, the sun has hardly risen each day upon the scene until some ostrich-like production, deposited in the night, hatches forth another unfledged candidate for religious honors.

Curious creatures many of them are! With *prima facie* evidence of a purpose to fly, they yet sport mere germs of wings; and, living in the desert wastes of wild speculation and conjecture, they, when attacked, generally imagine themselves impregnably defended when their very small amount of brains is hidden by the shifting sand of a technical quibble, or some high sounding but meaningless concatenation of words.

Again, this is an age of *faith*. Never were men and women so ready,—nay, never were they known to be so eagerly pining, and yearning, and aching to believe—something. Mr. Moody frequently alludes to the people who "are living on what they don't believe." He rather mistakes the indications. Very applicable to a past generation, his words do not so well describe this present day of 1894. Now, everybody believes. Everybody is in hot haste to believe. It is almost incredible to what an extent this mania for believing has gone. The daily attitude of our mentally active citizen appears to be described in the anxious inquiry, "Isn't there something new for me to believe to-day? I am just perishing to believe." No sooner is a "fad" presented than believers multiply like the shoals of herring and cod off our coast; and every fish immediately begins to spawn with such surprising fertility that one is prompted to wonder whether the mental waters will be able to afford sea room for the innumerable progeny.]

And this is the age of *creeds*. Oh! yes it is. Whenever you hear a modern Athenian stoutly maintaining his disbelief in the "creeds," just tack to windward, and coming up alongside his craft with a fair breeze, ask him to show you his own special chart of the coast, and outline his particular course, and you will speedily have another "creed" to add to the unlimited list. And the more violent his denunciation of other creeds, the more specious will be his pleading for his own darling creation.

I believe in science; I believe in broadgauge Christianity; I believe in humanitarianism; I believe in the electrical affinities of mental spheres; I believe in Theosophy; I, in mental science; I, in Esoteric Buddhism; I, in Occultism; and when one is so far gone that he really has no faith at all, he snatches up the old bell-mouthed blunderbuss of the infidel and fires a scattering volley over the whole creation at once in the vague phrase, "I believe in the Truth!"

Amid all this clatter there is not much room for the occasional voice that firmly declares, "I believe in God, and in Jesus Christ, His only Son, our Lord!"

Suppose a prophet had appeared in these United States at the close of the Rebellion, and had uttered this prediction: That, in less than a quarter of a century, thousands of educated men and women in this country, England, Europe, and India, would become outspoken advocates of Buddhism, that some phase of the despised heathen religions would secure more converts in Europe and America in twenty years than our religion has secured in the east in a century; that refined and educated Englishmen and Americans would teach and believe that man's soul passes through an infinity of incarnations or transmigrations, and that by becoming an adept through fasting, absolute continence ("forbidding to marry"), and the refusal to eat animal food ("commanding to abstain from meats." I. Timothy ii.), a man may be able to "recover the recollection of his previous incarnations"; that they would talk of "astral spirits" and "compel their souls" to go to any part of the universe at will, *a la* mesmeric *media;* that they would sink the Eternal Son of God to a level with a vast crowd of Christs, or those who have, in any age, "suffered for humanity"; that they would deny utterly the vicarious atonement and scoff at the blood, prating of a general " at-one-ment " with the supreme powers of the universe, *attained* by discipline and the knowledge of the truth, instead of *obtained* as a free gift; that they would proclaim to the world that the Bible is a very limited and much adulterated record of truth, not able to stand the tests of "higher criticism," and that the real custodians of the deeper mysteries have been not the prophets, not the Apostles, not Jesus Christ, but the disciples and priests of Buddha, and especially a certain set of mystics avowed to be secluded in the mountains of Thibet, only to be found and approached by an initiate; that they would revive and rehash the philosophies of the Rosicrucians, the Fire Worshippers, the Stoics, the Gnostics, and other ancient errors, mixing in a liberal supply of the old Canaanitish worship of

Plate 3.   THE RALLY.

"the host of heaven" (referring in Scripture to the gods, or demons); that they would prate of "spiritual affinities" between men and women, outside the marriage relation; write and talk of the "exaltation of woman," and the advent of a "female messiah," or "the second Eve," who is to save the world; that they should darkly whisper of a strange intercourse with the spirit world, of a possibility for women, and perhaps for some men, enjoying a sexual gratification with unseen beings, thus reviving the frightful sins of Canaan, and emphasize this teaching by the actual ceremonial marriage of a woman to a "spirit lover" in these United States; that they would start publication houses under the name of "culture," and issue books professing to be the depositories of all truth as preserved by the mystics; that esoteric (hidden) religion would be held up as vastly superior to the simple exoteric (open) religion of the cross, intelligible to a child as well as to the scholar; that they would openly publish and commend the practice of astrology, and even the "occult" or "black art" of the middle ages; and that they would find a crop of disciples ready to hand eager to believe all this and more in Boston, New York, Philadelphia, and London, well! —

If such a prophet had appeared, and so spoken twenty-five years ago, who would have done him honor? Who could have been expected to believe such a prediction? Yet all these things have actually come to pass in this century of grace, and in this "enlightened" land of ours.

But in opposition to all this, what has been done? What has Christianity to say? Can the theologians of our day present any answer to the charges of conflict between science and the Bible? It must be admitted that, too generally, the answers given have been dogmatic rather than reasonable. In fact they are frequently *bull-dogmatic*,—a mere tenacious holding on to a faith, without any disposition or ability to meet the difficulties raised by the other side. But this does not in the least prove that a proper answer is impossible. The presence of a thousand men, utterly ignorant of the art of boxing, is no proof of the nonexistence of a gifted pugilist; and let us remember that very few individuals anywhere know anything of fencing, either with sword or tongue. It is a fact not generally grasped that true logicians are about as rare as skillful fencers; and no better evidence can be given of a lack of logical equipment than the slur cast upon a truth simply because it is not ably defended. We take Mr. Huxley's proposition, that "one objection unremoved is as fatal to a theory as five hundred," and make "unremoved" equivalent to "unremovable."

But suppose it be possible to meet all the so-called objections to the Bible record? Suppose the much disputed first chapters of Genesis can be shown to contain the *only thoroughly scientific* account of the creation yet written? Suppose the old difficulties of the mention of light and the stars before the sun is spoken of; the absence of rain in Eden; the sudden change in costume of our first parents; the long life of the antediluvians; the Noachian deluge; the nonexistence of the rainbow before that great catyclysm; the unexpected result of Noah's grape juice; the coming of the wind after the rain instead of before it, as now universally occurs; the singular mention of the seasons and of day and night, that they "should not cease"; suppose all these can be explained? Nay, more. Suppose a scientist takes his position upon the Nebular Hypothesis and the great law of gravitation, and, standing under the wing of inflexible, admitted law, *demonstrates*, even to a nontechnical audience, that every one of these supposed contradictions is a great scientific necessity to the truth of the record; What then? Do not say it is impossible. Remember the "fencers," and recollect that a negative proposition cannot be proved.

It is no conceit whatever, but a profound conviction, based upon years of scientific study, as a student and professor of civil engineering and higher mathematics, while pursuing the investigation of the subjects herein mentioned, that leads the writer to firmly declare his ability to so explain these things to any intelligent audience. More than that, he has done so repeatedly (this book and its predecessor* being written in answer to an overwhelming demand that the lectures be pub-

---

* "Alpha and Omega, or The Birth and death of the World."

lished), and has always carried conviction to the majority of his hearers.

But how about the various religions alluded to? All have some truth mixed with them; and the logical answer can be found for all. Do you wish to know the mysteries of Spiritualism? Charles Foster's famous blood-writing on his arm, and the great Dr. Henry Slade's wonderful messages written between two slates held in open view? Well, the explanation is at hand. The writer is no medium, but he can do these things as well as their originators did them for him. (See a later chapter.) Do you ask concerning "Christian Science?" The reply is ready. The "Christian" is tested as to its consistency, and the "science" tested by inflexible law and logic. What of astrology? Many wonderful things, not generally known, along this branch of study, reveal some of the most surprising proofs of the truth of the Bible ever discovered. Sacred astronomy ought to be understood by the Christians of to-day; but like a great many weapons in their armory, it has been allowed to become rusty, and its very existence is not suspected by the vast majority. But so much is there here to know, that three or four whole lectures will not suffice to more than draw the outlines of the pictures.* And what shall be said of the field of sacred mathematics? Only this: that it is the most wonderful of all, and the most unanswerable; but into it, of course, the nonmathematical mind cannot be persuaded to follow.

The farthest thought from the writer's mind is to seek to puff any individual. He aims to extol the marvelous and infinitely exact TRUTH. That is all. Knowing that the answers exist, and that they can be made intelligible to any average audience of moderately educated people, he necessarily makes the assertion fearlessly. The truth can be defended, if you have the facts; and the facts are not generally very abstruse. "He who runs may read"; but most people refuse to run.

Nothing can exceed the floundering of scientists when endeavoring to bolster up an hypothesis based upon false assumptions. Nothing can be simpler than the unlocking of truth when you have the right key. Complexity is of man. (Simplicity is of God.)

* See "Alpha and Omega."

CHAPTER II.

Brief History of Spirit Manifestations.

SPIRITISM is a tremendous fact. Whatever people choose to believe or not to believe about the alleged manifestations of the spirit power, the thing itself — Spiritism — is undoubtedly a very present and prominent fact. The immense number of believers in Spiritism makes this fact of importance, for no man can sneer at the mere existence of a belief that enrolls millions of his fellow men among its votaries. He may laugh at the essence of the belief, but not at its existence. Bearing this in mind, anyone will see that the presence of ten millions of people in our own country, who are believers in Spiritism, is sufficient to enforce the statement that Spiritism is a tremendous fact. They, themselves, claimed this number of believers several years ago. I give it on their authority. But when we look abroad, and remember that the great majority of the inhabitants of heathen lands are ardent Spiritists; when we think of Africa with her millions of spirit and devil worshippers; of China with her dragon religion; and of the islands with their witch spells and various manifestations of the same general principle, we are compelled to admit the tremendous nature of this appalling fact, as we were not willing to do at a moment's notice.

The simple truth is that a very large majority of mankind is to be classed under the head of Spiritists in one form or another. This will be admitted by all who consider the facts in the case as hastily summed up in the above statements. For the purpose of our discussion and study I will divide the whole thing into two parts — the outward and the inward. With the first of these this chapter has alone to deal; and we will now hasten to read the history of Spiritism, ancient and modern.

Those who look to the Rochester rappings as

Plate 4. MICHAEL AND LUCIFER.

the origin of Spiritism are very much in the dark. (*The thing is as old as Eden.*) I may point to the serpent in Eden as the first "speaking medium" of which we have any knowledge. The "sons of God," who "took to themselves wives of the daughters of men" (Genesis vi. 2), were spirits, as we shall see at length further on. Many examples are found in the Old Testament of persons having dealings with spirits, as Jannes and Jambres, who withstood Moses, the Witch of Endor, and others; and in the New Testament such cases as Simon Magus, Elymas, the sorcerer, and the Sons of Sceva, serve to point this fact. But I leave all these for future study, and begin to trace the footsteps of Spiritism in later times.

In the thirteenth century sorcery was rampant at Narbonne. In 1300 Pope John XXII. complained of people who indulged in "rings" and "circles" and practiced the "magic arts." In 1484 Innocent VIII. issued a "bull" against sorcery in Germany. *In 1550, or thereabouts, thirty thousand persons were executed in England for sorcery in various forms.* In 1576 Bessie Dunlap, of

Dalry, professed to be "controlled" by the spirit of one Thomas Reid, who was killed in the battle of Pinkie, November 10, 1547. In 1594 the French jails could not hold the people who were committed on the charge of sorcery. In 1599 Agnes Sympson told King James that she was a "healing medium."

About this time Pordage, an English preacher, founded the "Philadelphian" society, and later the "Angelic Brethren." They claimed to see spirits, and to have messages from them. At Lund some of the nuns became affected and "wrote miraculously" at the dictation of the spirits.

In 1612 occurred the famous manifestations at the house of the Rev. Mr. Perreaud, in Burgundy. Curtains were drawn violently away from the bed, just after the occupants had retired, and in the full light of the candles. Knocks of the most violent description abounded. Many articles were thrown about the rooms.

The elders of the church instituted the most careful watch, but the manifestations went on just the same. The spirits would sing, and cry, and pray the Lord's Prayer, and repeat the Ten Commandments. The candlestick was snatched from the servant's hand, leaving the candle in her fingers. No trick or fraud was at any time detected in connection with these remarkable occurrences.

In 1680 came the wonderful excitement in this country. The fame of the Salem witches has been sounded far and wide, but very few are aware of the amount of sober evidence on the subject, tending to establish the occurrence of unaccountable phenomena. To those who think of Cotton Mather and his associates as a superstitious set of fools it may be a matter of surprise to be assured that the most startling things occurred in the very presence of too many witnesses to set it all aside with a shake of the head. Girls passed right through the air. They talked in any language, though when out of the trance they knew none except their mother tongue. One medium paraphrased the Psalms in such fine language as to amaze her auditors. Another was raised from the floor and held for a considerable time actually suspended without any support. All these and many other extraordinary incidents were witnessed to by the most reliable people, in a way to make us doubt all evidence whatever, if it was an entire delusion. Of course we are familiar with the fact that many of these poor creatures were executed during the excitement that prevailed.

The year 1716 saw the most famous manifestations of all, the "Epworth Rappings." These occurred at the home of the father of John and Charles Wesley, the founders of Methodism. No sane man can read the mass of evidence on this topic without experiencing some very queer feelings. If evidence establishes anything at all, then it is certain that a large number of most unaccountable things occurred during these manifestations. Knocks were heard in all parts of the house, and at all hours. The cradle with the baby in it began suddenly to rock violently. The sleeping children broke out into profuse sweats and moaned in their sleep. The wooden trencher on the supper table spun and danced of its own accord, before their eyes. Mr. Wesley was met at his

Plate 5. THE LAST DEFEAT.

more properly originated; but my readers will see from the hasty sketch given already that this was by no means the beginning of the spirit performances, as has been so commonly supposed. As to the genuineness of these later "raps," I will simply refer to the fact that Mrs. Margaret Fox Kane, the girl who began the rapping at Rochester, has been on the stage in 1890 relating how she produced the raps with the joints of her knee and great toe, and finding the people alarmed, continued the thing for her own amusement at first, and later became wedded to it on account of the widespread interest and excitement.*

Since that time (1848) the mediums have multiplied like the spawn of the herring. The whole land has been overrun by them. The genus has branched out into a great number of species. We now have speaking mediums, seeing mediums, tipping mediums, rapping mediums, painting, singing, dancing, healing, writing, materializing, and test mediums, etc.

*Still later, however, I am told she has stated that these letters and "expositions" were given for money, and that the explanations were not true. Evidently we must depend on other witnesses than the "medium."

The exceedingly trivial nature of all these manifestations has not escaped the comment of the leading Spiritists themselves. Mr. A. R. Wallace, in endeavoring to account for it, remarks that most people are very commonplace, and that therefore the majority of the manifestations are commonplace. A leading Spiritist of England recently told Lady Sandhurst that ' the Spiritualists of England are about the poorest lot of creatures that God ever made." But it certainly seems strange that among all the spirits of the dear departed none have ever risen above the low plane of these absurdly trivial tricks. Even when quoting from Homer and Shakespeare the spooks do not seem to have the slightest idea of the fitness of things. A leading Spiritist sent Mr. Stead, the editor of *The Review of Reviews*, the following, as coming to him from Homer himself. It is descriptive of the youth of Shakespeare, and was narrated by his daughter Susanna: —

> To brook for eels he oft did hie,
> But fonder was of pigeon pie.
> Planted he there that thriving tree,
> Bought he this box of birch for me.

more properly originated; but my readers will see from the hasty sketch given already that this was by no means the beginning of the spirit performances, as has been so commonly supposed. As to the genuineness of these later "raps," I will simply refer to the fact that Mrs. Margaret Fox Kane, the girl who began the rapping at Rochester, has been on the stage in 1890 relating how she produced the raps with the joints of her knee and great toe, and finding the people alarmed, continued the thing for her own amusement at first, and later became wedded to it on account of the widespread interest and excitement.*

Since that time (1848) the mediums have multiplied like the spawn of the herring. The whole land has been overrun by them. The genus has branched out into a great number of species. We now have speaking mediums, seeing mediums, tipping mediums, rapping mediums, painting, singing, dancing, healing, writing, materializing, and test mediums, etc.

*Still later, however, I am told she has stated that these letters and "expositions" were given for money, and that the explanations were not true. Evidently we must depend on other witnesses than the "medium."

The exceedingly trivial nature of all these manifestations has not escaped the comment of the leading Spiritists themselves. Mr. A. R. Wallace, in endeavoring to account for it, remarks that most people are very commonplace, and that therefore the majority of the manifestations are commonplace. A leading Spiritist of England recently told Lady Sandhurst that ' the Spiritualists of England are about the poorest lot of creatures that God ever made." But it certainly seems strange that among all the spirits of the dear departed none have ever risen above the low plane of these absurdly trivial tricks. Even when quoting from Homer and Shakespeare the spooks do not seem to have the slightest idea of the fitness of things. A leading Spiritist sent Mr. Stead, the editor of *The Review of Reviews*, the following, as coming to him from Homer himself. It is descriptive of the youth of Shakespeare, and was narrated by his daughter Susanna:—

> To brook for eels he oft did hie,
> But fonder was of pigeon pie.
> Planted he there that thriving tree,
> Bought he this box of birch for me.

Old "Jasper" with his pony brown,
Which bore him off to Warwick town,
"Harry," his dog, has long been dead,
And "Putsey," too, Susanna said.

. . . .

He and his mate one night did hie
To where a neighbor's pig did lie.
One gashed his throat with pigment red,
And one with white "foamed" mouth and head.
Next day the boys and girls did shout
To see the monster walk about.
"A sickening sight! Why aint it dead?
The pig's half killed!" the people said.

When Mr. Stead ventured to suggest that this might cause the enemy to blaspheme, the correspondent indignantly replied that he considered the "internal evidences afforded by the poem were sufficiently convincing." In this opinion Mr. Stead undoubtedly agreed with him.

I can but remark the amazing difference between such miserably little things and the majestic miracles of the Bible, — the cripples restored, the sick made whole, the dead brought back to life, the bread created for thousands in an hour, the sea divided, the thunder and hail, the mighty earthquakes, and the resurrection and ascension of

Jesus. And yet most of the people who accept the incredibly foolish tests of Spiritism are the first to object to the evidences, internal or external, of the almighty hand of God himself in the affairs of men. Camels are always easier to swallow than gnats.

CHAPTER III.

Spiritism — Its Outer Frauds.

MANY honest investigators believe that the whole of Spiritualism is nothing but one gigantic trick, or rather repetition of small tricks. Certain it is that trick has played, and does now play, a very important part in the outward show of the matter. This is not the assertion of the opposers of Spiritism, but the frank statement of its leading men. That there may be no possible mistake on this point I will quote from the authorities.

Joel Tiffany, a leading Spiritist, says: "The point to which I want to call your attention is the almost universal fact that when a medium, devoted to external manifestations, is under the control of

Plate 6.   THE SPIRIT OF VILE FRAUD.

his presiding spirit, he is under an influence to deceive, to cheat, that is well-nigh irresistible." (Lectures, p. 122.) He says he has seen this with the most powerful mediums in the world. As an explanation he speaks of breathing through an onion stalk, by which performance the breath acquires the odor of the stalk; and then likens this to the transmission of the spirit messages through the medium. Certainly this is terribly hard on the poor mediums, coming as it does from their own friend.

In Mr. Stead's search for an honest materializing medium, he was assured by the leading Spiritists of England that there was not a single person in the whole United Kingdom, accustomed to give that class of manifestation, whose name had not been coupled with fraud, except one woman whom he failed to meet. This from the Spiritists themselves.

The most conclusive statement on this subject, and the one which gives the real secret of the thing, is an utterance in the well-known Spiritist magazine called the *Banner of Light*, in October,

1878. The writer states that it is the result of years of the most careful study, thought, observation, and investigation. He says: "To my mind fraud has the deepest significance. In connection with Spiritualism's present *status* I regard it as essential. It is the safety valve; the touchstone of Spiritualism. I say it without fear of contradiction, take fraud out of Spiritualism and it would dash to pieces in twelve months. You would deprive it of its safety valve. Instead of curses, it (fraud) should receive blessings. The office of public mediumship is to divert the attention of the masses from Spiritualism *per se*. It is ever on the stage. It keeps the ignorant world amused. It is the butt of science. It provokes the Christian's mirth. It draws the ridicule of the rationalist and the sneers of the skeptic. But in the meantime, behind the scenes, in ten thousand homes, the cause goes right on through ten thousand private mediums."

I call special attention to this last sentence. It is most terribly true, as we will see later. Possibly the progress of Christianity may have something to do with the presence of so much trick in Spiritism. From their magazine, *Mind and Matter*, for May 8, 1880, see the following. Advanced spiritualists realize that the palmy days of Spiritism were before the Gospel light appeared, and the editor speaks thus: "Under the leadership and guidance of the learned Brahmins of India, the Mongolian people had advanced to a state of spiritual growth that has never since been attained by the most cultivated and enlightened nations of the world. Following in their wake the Magi of Western Asia had led the people, who recognized their spiritual acquirements, to a point that bordered on the sublime. Egypt in turn received the glowing light of spiritual knowledge as it rolled on its westward course. . . . . Such was the state of the world at the commencement of the so-called Christian era. The sun of Spiritualism had then acquired such power as to promise to dispel the fast disappearing clouds of superstition, ignorance, and selfishness, which had so long enveloped the world of humanity. From Eastern Asia to Western Europe, from the Arctic

Ocean to the burning sands of Ethiopia, Spiritualism gave promise of a glorious and universal day. . . . . The barriers that had been raised to obstruct the outflow of spirit communion were rapidly giving way, and the stream of knowledge was broadening and widening so rapidly as to promise ere long to satisfy every thirsting soul. Such was the propitious outlook at that period of the world's history. . . . . Step by step Christianity advanced, and as it did so, step by step the torch of Spiritualism receded, until hardly a flickering ray from it could be perceived amid the deep darkness. . . . . For more than eighteen hundred years has the so-called Christian church stood between mortals and spirits [*mark this statement well for later chapters*] barring all chance for progress and growth. It stands to-day as complete a barrier to human progress as it did eighteen hundred years ago."

The importance of these words cannot be overestimated. They contain more truth than the writer knew or intended. But the thought which prompted their introduction here was to show that

Plate 7. THE GENIUS OF FABLE.

such opposition on the part of Christianity, at a time when the supernatural side of Spiritism was more prominent and powerful than ever before, had the effect of developing the trick and fraud as a substitute for the real. The tricks of Spiritism, as practiced to-day, are the merest imitations of sleight of hand. They never equal the best performances of the professors of that art. There is no sort of doubt on this point in the mind of any intelligent investigator, who has been properly equipped for his work.

When the famous Charles Foster appeared about 1872, he astonished the world for a time with his clever reading of folded papers, and his showing the initials of dead friends of his visitors written in blood on his arm. Later Dr. Henry Slade produced his famous slate writing in England and on the continent, and finally held his protracted seances with the professors of Leipsic University. As a result of these sittings, Professor Zollner wrote a book called "Transcendental Physics," in which he attempted to argue for a supposed "fourth dimension in space," which the spirits were able to utilize in order to accomplish Slade's wonders. In this country Rev. Joseph Cook took up these reported marvels, and on his famous Boston Monday platform committed himself to an acceptance of them as genuine. He stated that he had talked with able professors of legerdemain, and that all agreed that they could not produce or explain such marvels as those wrought by Dr. Slade. Mr. Cook even went so far as to compare the reported passing of a shell through a table (one of Slade's tricks with the Germans — a most elementary sleight of hand trick, by the way) with the miracle of Jesus passing through the door to meet with his disciples after his resurrection.

At that time I had not seen Dr. Slade, but I wrote to Mr. Cook that if he would visit Mr. Maskelyne, at Egyptian Hall in London, the latter would reproduce and explain all the manifestations actually done by Dr. Slade. Mr. Cook replied, thanking me for my note, but I do not know whether he ever profited by the suggestion. Some time after this I myself was able to secure two sittings with Dr. Slade, in company with a friend — an expert *prestidigitateur*. I am quite well versed in the mysteries of the art myself, and between us we had not the smallest difficulty in detecting the redoubtable doctor in all his performances. In my public lectures, from which this book has grown, I repeat for my audiences these famous tricks of the two notorious mediums above mentioned. I can do them quite as well as they did them for me, and in just the same way employed by them. Several years ago I wrote up these performances in the *Microcosm*, but will now give a brief sketch of the chief tricks.

Foster's reading of folded papers was accomplished in this wise: He sat at one side of a small table. The visitors wrote several names on slips of soft paper, and folded the same. He did not see the writing, nor watch the writers. When all were written he took up one and another of the papers and pressed them to his forehead, meanwhile keeping up earnest talk about the marvels of Spiritism. It was a very simple matter to hold one paper in the palm of the hand and naturally drop the hand into the lap, hidden by the table from the visitors. Here the right hand easily unrolled the paper while Foster pretended to talk to a spirit whom he located to one side. Talking earnestly to this spook, he leaned over to the right, and glancing towards his knee under the edge of the table, read the name on the paper. A moment sufficed to refold the paper and conceal it in the palm of the hand, and then he proceeded to describe the name of the spirit in the most striking language he could bring to bear. If the name happened to be a well-known personage, like Brigham Young for example, he would seize on the prominent characteristics of the individual in his description. Finally the name was announced to the startled writer.

This foolishness was repeated, and then, having obtained another name in the same way, Foster suggested writing a question for the spirits to answer. While the visitor was busy at this he seized the opportunity to pull up his sleeve and write the initials of the last name (secured from a paper) on his wrist. For this he used a piece of ordinary

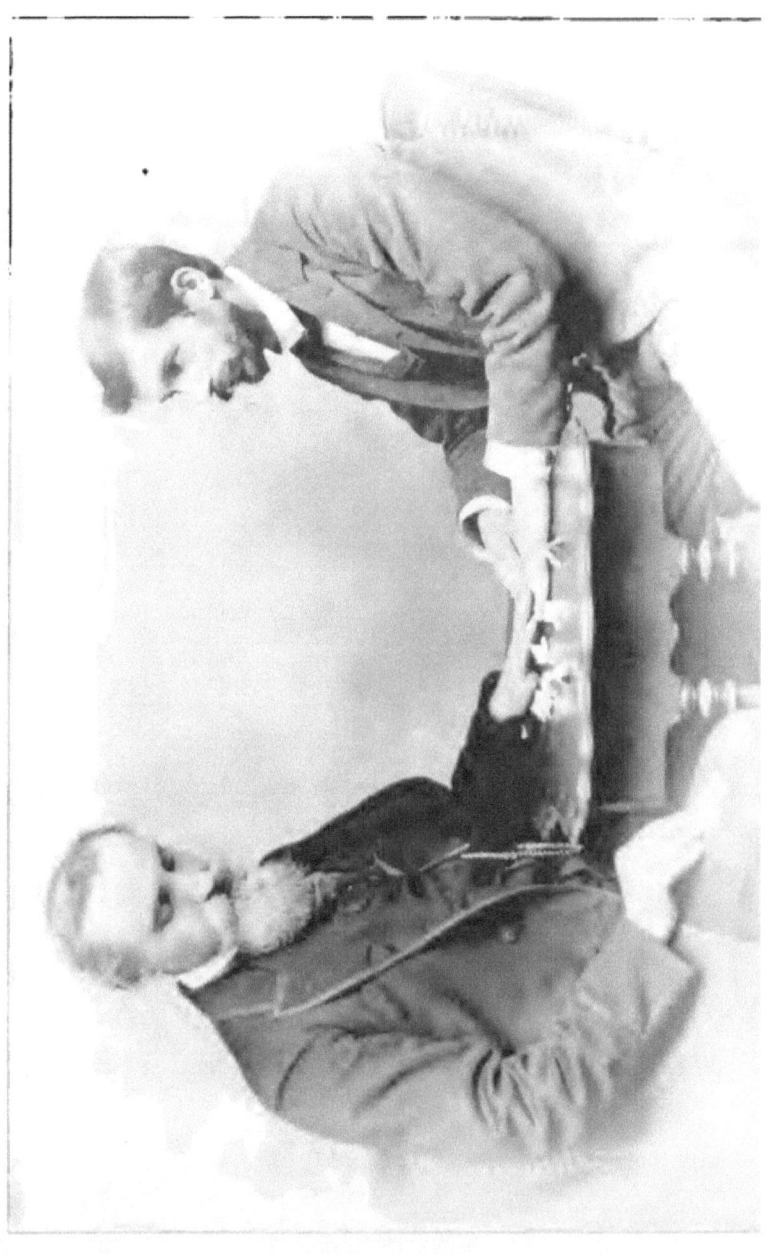

red paint, or occasionally scratched his skin with a sharp diamond ring. Presently he would go through a lot of acting, complaining of pain, etc., and declaring that a spirit insisted on writing his name on his arm in blood. Then suddenly pulling up his sleeve he showed the astounded visitor the wet red letters of the very name he had written and folded up. The effect was sometimes tremendous. The questions written were read and answered in the same way. This trick was Foster's stock in trade. I have met people who claim that he told them things about themselves that were yet future, but for me he only performed these absurd tricks in the manner described.

Dr. Slade proceeded in this manner: On a small table near him was a pile of common slates. One of them he handed to me for inspection. A second he showed me, but did not let me handle. (The uninitiated in sleight would not notice this.) He took a sponge and carefully wiped both sides of the slate he held and allowed me to clean the other. His slate was then placed on the table, a small piece of pencil laid on it, and my slate on top of that. We joined hands in the middle of the table while Slade talked glibly of spirits, and asked them if they would write on the slates. As he asked this question, he placed the slates partly under the table, and as a knock was heard, giving assent to his question, he brought the slates on top of the table and opened them to our inspection, then placed another piece of pencil on my slate, put his slate on top (it had been underneath—another point the ordinary observer would never notice), and holding the two right under my friend's chin, told us to listen to the writing. We distinctly heard a sound like that caused by a slate pencil. He then handed the slates to my friend, and said, "Open them and see what they have written." When taken apart, a long message was written on one of them. This, with slight variations, is the basis of all Slade's famous tricks.

The explanation is exceedingly simple. The second slate, which he did not allow us to touch, had the message already written upon it, and carefully covered with a neatly fitting piece of black cardboard. When he passed the slates under the

Plate 9. The Blood Writing.

table, asking the spirits if they would write, he dropped this cardboard in his lap, thus leaving the writing exposed, but on the under side of the slate. Returning the slates to the table, he lifted the upper one "to show us there was nothing there," and then placed the lower one on top, thus bringing the message between the slates, where it was wanted. Of course, then all that was necessary was to hold the slates anywhere, as on my friend's breast, and to gently scratch with his finger nail on the hidden side, thus making the sound like writing, and then to allow us to open the slates and see what was written.

In receiving the statement that this is all there is to the wonderful slate writing, the reader must bear in mind the very effective talking of the medium. Dr. Slade is one of the most accomplished actors to be met with anywhere, and looks you in the eye with the most childlike innocence, while he affects to be as surprised as you at the wonderful things done by the spirits. The uninitiated person is astonished and awed in spite of his incredulity, and this feeling grows with every new trick, and the skillful talk of the impostor, until the person becomes so amazed and generally confused that the most trivial things can be done without any fear of detection. Thus it was that Dr. Slade succeeded in fooling the learned Germans to so great an extent. He would not have succeeded half so well with an audience of country bumpkins whose eyes had been trained in the open fields, and were accustomed to catch every movement about them.*

In my own lectures, I easily go beyond these tricks of the redoubtable doctor, and show how readily the best of them can be outdone by a little real sleight of hand. (Of course, no one must believe the generally vague reports of marvelous things done by such mediums, when such reports come from anyone not versed in the trickery just described. All such evidence is absolutely worthless, for the simple reason that the persons giving it do not know where to look, nor how to judge of the movements of the medium, and are therefore not competent witnesses.

* For more points on the German seances, see further on.

The various "cabinet" tricks are all as easily explained. The medium allows himself to be tied by a committee. After a good while, by skillful squirming, he manages to get loose. He then ties himself "in order to expedite matters," and the committee pronounces the knots to be first class. They are *first-class frauds.* By simply leaning in a certain direction, they are loosened so that the hands can be instantly withdrawn and as quickly replaced. In this way all that kind of trick is managed. The famous "materializations" are arranged by having the drapery for the various spirits hidden in some part of the cabinet, or to be reached through an ingeniously concealed door; the medium enters the cabinet, the lights are lowered, and the various transformations readily effected. If any bold enemy turns on the lights or seizes the spirit, finding it to be the medium, the faithful are taught that this is to be expected, for the dematerialization must necessarily leave only the human medium. This form of manifestation has been so often detected that it has become rare. A skillful use of mirrors, at some expense in the arranging, enables the medium to perform some astonishing materializations. Professor Kellar, the magician, does some excellent work in this line.

The table tippers and trance writers make a great deal of money out of their dupes. The thing is very easy, the chief requisite being an unlimited amount of cheek, joined with an utter disregard of the punishment promised to all liars.

The "test mediums" sometimes display a faculty that cannot be explained by any of these tricks, but must be dealt with on psychological grounds. Mr. John Slater will tell twenty people in one audience trivial things that they have said or done that day, and name their dead relatives without any writing or questions, etc. He is a first-class mind reader, of the Bishop and Tyndall type. Only this, and nothing more. Passing near the susceptible persons in his audience, he easily catches some thought from their minds. Then he begins to talk about it, and that makes the person addressed think the more intently upon it. This helps the mind reader to get more details;

and if the thing does not appear to work well, he runs to the individual, and takes hold of his hand, sometimes pressing the hand to his brow. In this way he is enabled to read the thought as do the men referred to, who make no claim to any supernatural force whatever. I have seen Tyndall instantly read a long number from the mind of a gentleman by simply taking hold of his hand while the gentleman thought intently of it; and again have seen him, while completely blindfolded, driving a double team furiously through the crowded streets of San Francisco, without coming into collision with the vehicles or cable cars, guided only by the thought of a gentleman sitting by his side and touching his wrist. This power is akin to that displayed by the somnambulist, and needs no spirits to explain it. It is wonderful, truly, but not at all supernatural. When possessed by an unscrupulous medium, of course a great deal can be made out of it, and thousands of persons effectually duped. Fortunately very few mediums have this faculty so well developed as Mr. Slater, while men like Bishop and Tyndall scorn to make capital by perjuring themselves in ascribing it to spiritualistic influences.

One of the most interesting manifestations of Spiritualism is that of "spirit photography." A person sits for a picture, and when the negative is developed there appears upon it the shadowy face and form of a spirit, generally some one connected with the sitter by relationship. Leading articles upon this subject have found place in the magazines, notably two in the *Illustrated Californian*, one written for and the other against the genuineness of the photographs.

At once it may be said that there are several ways in which a faint shadowy picture may be produced upon a negative so as to seem to appear behind the sitter or in front of him, allowing him to be seen through the shadow or specter. It is not necessary to give all the details, except to say that the faint negative of the spirit photograph may be arranged so as to print simultaneously with the regular one, the two appearing on the same finished picture. There are other ways in which the shadow may be made to show upon the glass plate

Plate II.   SPIRIT PHOTOGRAPHY.

or negative itself, and photographers have no difficulty in producing such effects. In the articles mentioned the writer who upholds the truth of the matter on the spiritualistic side himself admits that these ways exist and even says he is acquainted with them; but he insists that in his experience with the photographer, Mumler, and others, he is certain that such deceptions were not practiced.

Mumler himself once gave a sworn testimony in which he declared most solemnly that he never practiced any of the methods of deception, but that the spooks appeared upon his negative of their own free will at all times. Dr. Clarke, the writer of the *Californian* article, insists that the evidence given in his article is conclusive, and that none stronger could be devised. To this we demur most decidedly. Dr. A. Wilford Hall recently made a very tempting offer to the leading advocates of Spiritualism in New York to produce spirit photographs under perfectly fair and practicable conditions, but the offer remains unaccepted. Many others have gone into the investigation with all honesty of purpose only to be convinced that fraud, and fraud alone, ruled in the matter. The statements of Dr. Clarke about his pictures seem very strong, but the scientific investigator discovers several crucial points where his account of precautions is incomplete, and the skillful detector of deceit is ready with suggestions and explanations at once. Even if some of these men may be admitted honest, we are irresistibly reminded of the words of the Spiritualist, Joel Tiffany, that a Spiritualist when under the control of his presiding spirit, is "under an influence to deceive and cheat that is well-nigh irresistible."

Dr. Clarke says that the pictures given with his article were "instantly recognized." Unless the originals were vastly clearer than the magazine prints, it is certain that one or two of them might be easily "recognized" by anybody, for they are so dim and uncertain in outline that a ready imagination would find no difficulty in seeing a resemblance to some friend. On the whole we conclude that the evidence so far presented for spirit photography is very slim indeed. In fact it hardly deserves a place at all in the consideration of the matter. Most of the spirit photographers have confessed to fraud in the production of their negatives, and of the few who have not, not one has ever stood the rigid scientific and reasonable tests proposed by Dr. Hall and others during the last few years.

This covers the field of the outer tricks pretty thoroughly in so far as the overwhelming majority of all public tests, even by the most noted mediums is concerned. There remains however a small number of phenomena, supported by rather exceptional testimony, which must be fairly represented before proceeding farther. But for these, other chapters are necessary.

CHAPTER IV

Transcendental Physics.

To be perfectly fair towards your opponent is a cardinal principle in all reasonably conducted debate; and, with this in mind, I must give special attention to the extraordinary experiments carried on at Leipsic, during the years 1877, 1878, by four or five professors in the great university, in conjunction with Dr. Henry Slade. The character and reputation of the gentlemen, and the fact that nearly all the experiments were reported as performed in their own private houses, in the broad daylight, under the most severe conditions, coupled with the fact that many of the tests were of such a nature as to allow the results to be preserved, defying all attempts to satisfactorily explain them (if they were correctly reported), place this series of performances on a different plane from those already described. I will endeavor to give as clear a description as possible of these remarkable seances, with whatever theoretical explanation occurs to me, and fairly indicate those for which no such solution seems possible.

The persons engaged in these investigations were Johann Carl Friedrich Zollner, professor of physical astronomy at Leipsic University, William Edward Weber, professor of physics, Gustave T. Fechner, professor of physics, and Scheiber, professor of mathematics. Besides these, Professor von Hoffmann and several others witnessed many of the tests.

The sitting room in Zollner's house was the place where the majority of the phenomena occurred. Slade was the guest of these gentlemen, and, Zollner says, no special money consideration entered into the arrangements. He, all along, declared himself to be as earnestly anxious to find out the truth as the professors themselves, and they testify to the gentlemanly character of his actions. It does not appear that these men were Spiritualists, but only that they were interested in the phenomena as such, and that Zollner thereby developed his theory that some beings may be acquainted with another "dimension in space" besides those of length, breadth, and thickness, on account of which they are able to perform what seems to us the miraculous.

Of course it is agreed at once that any creature who does not possess a sense belonging to other creatures, is utterly unable to comprehend things which are simple to them. A man born blind cannot possibly understand what we mean by colors. You cannot explain the distinctions to him, no matter how long you try to do so. He cannot even *think* in the sphere of color, but thinks of feelings and such sensations. So Zollner reasons that certain beings may have another sense by which they appreciate another dimension in space, and, by means of this, they can even pass a solid through a solid without rupturing either. When Joseph Cook compared Jesus' coming through the door into the room where the disciples were gathered with the passage of the shell through the table, as reported by Zollner, he accepted the latter as a true account, and merely meant to allude to the possible existence of a "law" for such occurrences.

(As a devout student of true science, I unhesitatingly lay down the postulate that all things are done according to law in this universe. Miracle merely steps on to a higher plane than that upon which man is able to walk, and uses laws which are entirely beyond his control, or even his knowledge. But that the laws exist, and that they are applied by divine power in miracle, no sensible reasoner will deny. With regard to the Leipsic phenomena, however, the very first thing asked is, "Did the tests really succeed as stated?" With some very natural reluctance I answer, that later developments seem to cast grave doubts upon the accuracy of the published descriptions, and we cannot feel easy in accepting the statements of Zollner's remarkable book. The very gentlemen who were with him now utterly fail to support this extraordinary account in many most important particulars.

I have read the book as carefully as possible, and see no difficulty in accounting for a great deal on the principles I have described. The slates were constantly used, but in different ways. One of the most remarkable in Professor's Zollner's eyes, was when he, Zollner, took both slates in his own right hand, holding one of them on the top of the table, near the edge, and the other just under the table, so that his right hand grasped the two slates, one above and the other under the table, the board of the table top being between them. Both of Slade's hands were on top of the table, and in contact with the left hand of Professor Zollner, the room being flooded with daylight. A small piece of pencil was laid on the table under the upper slate. The sound of writing was heard, and when Zollner removed the slates, which he did without Slade touching either of them, writing was found, not under the upper slate, where the pencil was, but on the upper surface of the under slate, as though the pencil had written through the table.

As an easy solution, I suggest the following:

Plate 12.   HELIODORUS PUNISHED IN THE TEMPLE.

While Zollner alone handled the slates during the trick, yet Slade had handled them before, and himself gave them to Zollner, at the supposed beginning of the performance. I say the "supposed" beginning, because in reality it had begun before, possibly before Slade came to the room at all. It was a very simple thing to write a message on a slate, using a certain form of sympathetic ink that would not begin to show until it was moistened. This prepared slate was handed to Zollner with a second one, and he was allowed to wash both of them with a sponge handed him by Slade. This sponge contained either water alone, or with some solution capable of developing the ink on the slate. (I give no details here, as there is no use furnishing frauds with ammunition for their depredations on mankind.) No time was lost after the washing in arranging the slates above and beneath the table, and the act proceeded. Slade talked enough to occupy the time while the developed ink dried, and assumed a whitish color near enough to that of faint pencil marks to escape detection in ordinary hands, and meanwhile produced the sound of writing in one of the many ways open to his experienced mind. As both his hands were held by Zollner, it is probable that he made the sound by means of a bit of pencil, or any other hard substance, attached to his knee or foot, and gently scraped against the table top (underneath), or the leg of the table. Anyone familiar with the laws of acoustics will easily appreciate the ease with which one's attention may be directed to a certain point as the supposed location of a sound, when really it is being produced somewhere else. In this way Zollner readily thought the sound of writing came from the slates, the conducting power of the wood of the table making the delusion effective. Of course, when he removed the slates, the writing was there, and in this case, under the table, thus giving color to the ready remark of Slade that the spirits had written through the wood of the table top.

Zollner's pocket knife was laid upon the slate, and the latter passed under the table when the knife was several times projected up in the air, falling on the table, and with the blade open. I mention this simply because Slade produced the same phenomenon with me, using the long pencil instead of a knife. Just as the slate was passing under the table the pencil was thrown out and up, so as to fall on the table or in my lap. Beyond any doubt whatever Slade himself threw the pencil by a dexterous twist of the wrist,--a feat which I easily accomplished after two or three trials.

Experiments were performed with the magnetic compass. The medium passed his hand over the glass, and no effect followed. Immediately on repeating the passes, the needle was violently agitated, even circling completely around in the box. It would not take a sleight of hand performer long to accomplish this feat, by the simple transference of a piece of iron from one hand to the other, concealing it in the palm, as is so constantly done, and the effects mentioned would follow.

For another class of tests I can offer a possible, though not a likely solution. I refer to those experiments during which some article suddenly disappeared from sight altogether and presently reappeared. Zollner mentions one very extraordinary effect of this kind. A round-top table was gently laid on its side, with the leg (a central one with feet) under the table on which his and Slade's hands were resting. It was placed thus by the spirits, while Zollner looked on. After awhile he looked under the larger table, and the round one had entirely disappeared. Furthermore, it was not in the room at all. Remembering that this occurred in the broad daylight, in his own sitting room, and that Slade's hands never left the table for a moment, the full force of the test will be realized. Suddenly, in the midst of the astonishment caused by such an event, the missing table appeared in the air, upside down, and near the ceiling, floating over the other table. Zollner and Slade both dodged, but were hit on the head and shoulder by the round table as it fell upon the larger one. Zollner says he felt the bruise for several days.

During one of my own sittings with Slade he mentioned the fact that articles sometimes disappeared, and on my expressing a great desire to witness such a phenomenon, he kindly asked his spirits to oblige us by removing a small paper box which he placed on top of a slate, when he passed the slate beneath the table. At once he arose, exclaiming in apparent astonishment. "Why, I declare, it has gone!" We looked under the table and all about, but could find no trace of the missing box. Taking our seats again, the slate was passed under the table by Slade and immediately withdrawn, when the lost box was seen upon it as before. I need hardly say to the initiate in sleight of hand that we did not look for the box *under the slate*, which, while we searched, Slade kept in his hand. He simply turned the slate over and held the little box close to its under side by means of an extended finger. That was all; and so ridiculously simple was it that my friend and myself had great difficulty in restraining our real emotions.

But the floating table cannot be explained on any such hypothesis. I, however, offer the following as applicable to many such tests: An educated American, recently in India, witnessed the tricks of one of the best traveling jugglers upon the street. The performer, a tall, black-eyed man, looked all around, catching every eye with his piercing glance, and then uncoiling a slender rope, threw the coil in the air, where it appeared to hook over an unseen support. He then called out, and was answered by a boy's voice, and after some jerking on the rope a leg fell down, then an arm, and so on till the entire members of the boy lay at his feet. He made passes over them, put them together, and lo! the youth revived, climbed up the rope, and disappeared whence he came, while the juggler recoiled the rope and "passed the hat," or something to that effect.

Next day the American went in quest of the same performer, accompanied by an artist and a man with a camera. The same performance was witnessed by the first, and was sketched by the second, who also saw precisely what the first did. But the negatives, taken rapidly by the photographer, showed the crowd, the Americans, the juggler, the rope in his hand, but no hanging rope, and no boy at all.

The explanation is irresistibly evident. The

practiced performer, by his keen glance, actually mesmerized the crowd, or most of it, — mesmerized the two Americans so that both saw the same things. Under his spell, as is common in such matters, the "subjects" saw what, and only what, the juggler made them see. But the little camera was not a "subject," and hence told only the strict truth. I remark that this is probably the solution of many of the otherwise unaccountable feats said to have been performed by Eastern jugglers in the presence of Europeans.

Now, I suggest the possibility that Dr. Slade secured such control of Professor Zollner, that he mesmerized him in a similar manner, and caused a table to disappear from his view, and again to appear over his head in the air. The bruise, or sensation of one, can be explained on the same basis. Remember that the things "seen" by a mesmerized "subject" are precisely as real and vivid to him as if actually occurring. I say I suggest this as possible, but in view of the other tests, of which I will now speak, it does not seem very likely, if they are correctly reported, that

Slade used mesmeric power at all. A few more tests, like the appearance of a "small reddish-brown hand" moving along the edge of the table, and touching one and another of the gentlemen, and of a large hand firmly gripping Zollner's arm until it caused pain, though occurring in the full light, might be explained in the same way, and it is possible this may essentially cover the majority of phenomena.

Let the reader particularly notice that the following is said to have occurred during Slade's first visit to Zollner's house, when he had certainly had no possible chance to arrange any effects with the furniture, even if those which were witnessed could have been brought about by trick. The gentlemen named were seated, with Slade, around a table, engaged in some tests with the slates. Suddenly a large bed, standing several feet away, and behind a strong screen, moved out about two feet from the wall, pushing the screen as it did so.

Slade's back was towards the bed, his hands on the table, and his legs crossed and fully visible. The tests were resumed, when without a warning the strong wooden screen alluded to was torn assunder with a loud crack, like that of a very large battery of Leyden jars. The part broken fell away from Slade, whose back was turned towards it at the time, and his hand and feet fully visible, as before. Of course, this feat was not mesmeric. The broken screen remained in evidence, and the nature of the performance may be better understood when we learn that the mechanical force necessary to tear assunder such wood is calculated to be about twenty thousand pounds.

While they stood looking on in wonder, Slade placed a slate, bought and washed by Zollner, on top of the table, with a little bit of pencil under it, and standing by the table, with his fingers pressed down on the slate, writing was heard by all, the slate lifted, and the message read: "It is not our intention to do harm, forgive what has happened."

I could readily offer a suggestion as to the manner in which this writing may have been done, but in the face of such astounding results it is hardly worth while, particularly when we recall that all this happened during the very first visit of the Doctor to Zollner's house, and that the torn screen still remains in witness.*

On another occasion while Zollner was talking to Slade, he and others suddenly saw his knife fly through the air and strike Professor Scheiber, who was standing ten feet distant from Slade, in the forehead. The scar was visible to all next day. Slade's back was turned towards Scheiber, and he could not possibly have thrown the knife without detection, as he and Zollner were standing together in the full light of the windows.

One of the best of Slade's tests with the Germans was that of tying knots in a piece of twine, both ends of which were brought together and sealed down on a card. The sealing was done by two of the professors with their own cord, cards, and seals, and afterwards brought by them to the seance. The looped ends of the cords were allowed to hang over the side of the table on Slade's side, while the card was held down on top and in plain view. Zollner states that both Slade's

---

* My comment on this and others as inexplicable is: Are the events recorded exactly? And why has Slade been unable ever since to reproduce these effects?

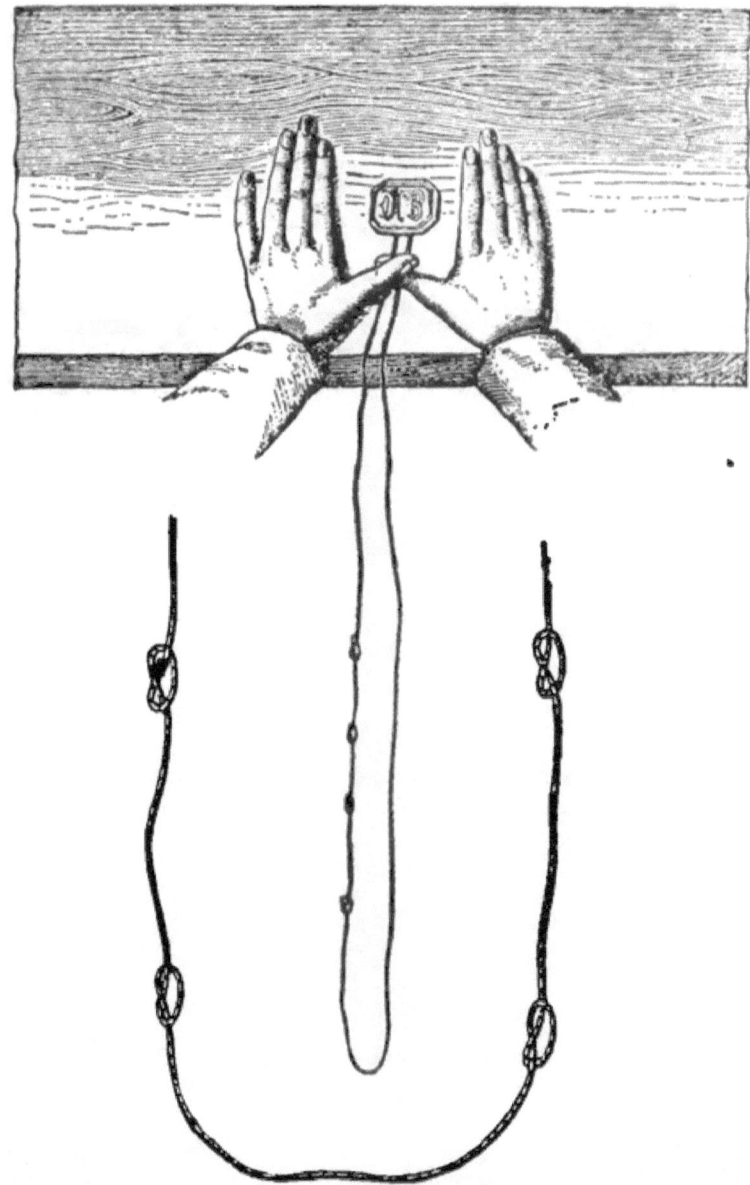

Plate 13.   KNOTS IN ENDLESS CORD.

hands were kept on top of the table, and that both his feet were visible all the time. Yet, in a few minutes the cord was laid on the table, and behold, three or four knots were tied in the unbroken string.

Every possible precaution, he says, was taken in this test, the looped cord never leaving Zollner's hand until laid on the table, and the hands of the medium remaining in full sight all the time. Two others were tied by Professor Weber. Of course, in this case, the results were permanent, and the cord has been preserved, with the seal intact. Yet Weber does not now speak with any positiveness.

Another remarkable result was obtained with a large bowl of flour, level full. This was set under the table, when a hand grasped Zollner's leg, and on examination all could plainly see the mark of the hand on his trousers, while in the flour was a deep imprint of a hand much larger than that of Slade. The latter gentleman's hands had never left the table during this test. Zollner kept the bowl with the imprint in the flour for many months as a proof of the result.

On another occasion a sheet of paper was covered with soot from a lamp, and laid on a board under the table. Suddenly the board was pushed out into the room, and there in the lampblack was the print of a naked human left foot. Slade was instantly examined, but his shoes and stockings were in place, and his foot proved to be at least an inch longer than the print. As usual, his hands were in plain view all the time. A reduced photograph of this paper has been retained.

So impressed were the professors by this test that Zollner made special preparation for a more difficult one. He procured a "book-slate," — that is, one with hinges connecting two slates, like the covers of a book. Without showing them to Slade, he lined the interior with paper covered with lamp black, closed the book, and bound it about with cords, carefully sealed. When it was shown to Slade the latter seemed to think it impossible for any prints to be obtained on the paper, but "asked the spirits" to attempt it, receiving the answer, "We will try."

To Zollner's surprise he was allowed to lay the

slates on his own lap beneath the table, in such a position that he could look down and see fully one half of them. All hands were then "linked with Slade's" for about five minutes, when Zollner felt two distinct downward pressures upon his lap. He opened the slates in full view of all present, and on one was the clear print of a right foot, and upon the other that of a left foot.*

But the most remarkable of all the tests with slates was the following: A large book-slate was bought, bound with strong cords, sealed with paper strips and stamped wax in four or five places. The frames fitted very closely together, so that even without the binding a sheet of paper could hardly have been forced between. Of course, after the binding and sealing no room remained for the insertion of any paper unless in very narrow strips. All this was arranged by the professors, without Dr. Slade seeing any of the preparations. Professor Wach had written on

---

* One gets the impression from the book that all the professors were present at most of the sittings. But they now say this is not so. Most of these tests were done in Zollner's presence alone, and Slade was allowed to dictate all conditions.

the strips of paper before they were pasted around the slates, so that this additional test could be applied when opened. If any one had torn the paper off and replaced it, he could not have fitted the writing together on the under side. In addition to the slates, a sheet of paper was laid on the top of the table, a small bit of graphite placed upon it, and then covered with another sheet of paper somewhat larger in size. The latter was done in the hope that writing would be obtained on the paper in lead pencil instead of on a slate. But this time a surprise was in store.

On raising the paper cover from the table the other sheet of paper and the bit of lead had disappeared. Not finding them anywhere, the use of the slate was resorted to, and the spirits wrote upon it that the missing paper would be found in the bound and sealed book-slate. Zollner did not open it, but carried it to the house of Professor Wach, who had written on the paper strips pasted about it, and allowed him to open it. Sure enough, there was the missing sheet of paper, smooth and uncreased, and bearing writing in lead pencil, asking if the investigators would not now believe in the "fourth dimension of space." The bit of lead was also within. Zollner points out the impossibility of inserting the sheet of paper in any way unless it had been folded up into a narrow strip so as to enter between the crossing bands of paper and cord. But it was found unfolded within the slates. It is needless to add that no "explanation" can be advanced for this phenomenon, *if it be correctly described.*

For the sake of variety I mention a few less remarkable tests. A large hand bell was laid on the floor by the side of the table, hands being all joined on top of the same. The bell was slowly and quietly pushed into Zollner's hand, which alone was held underneath. Slade's hands did not go out of sight.

Again Slade read easily marked sentences through two crossed Nicol's prisms, the effect of which is to absolutely cut off the light. He called this a "clairvoyant experiment." Of course this test presents no special difficulty for a mind reader like Mr. Tyndall.

At one time Professor Weber's coat was slowly unbuttoned, his gold watch taken from his pocket, and laid in his right hand beneath the table. All other hands were joined above the table. Slade's hands never left the table top, and the room was flooded with daylight.

Again, in the presence of three gentlemen, a book was placed on the slate beneath the table. In a moment it vanished, and could not be found in the room. Suddenly it fell from the ceiling, passing between the shades of the three-branched chandelier. This was repeated several times, the book striking Zollner on the ear from behind, while Slade sat in front of him. As against the mesmeric suggestion in this case, may be mentioned the fact that Slade asserted he saw lights in the upper part of the room, which assertion he also made when the round table floated in the air. But no one saw the lights except himself. If under a mesmeric influence it is not likely that the subjects would fail to see what the operator plainly told them was visible. I mention this to give fair play.

Two bands of soft leather were arranged in a way similar to the looped cord already described. The ends of both were sealed to cards, and the seals stamped by the professors. But these looped bands were suddenly passed through one another in the most intricate manner. They are still preserved, and the seals are unbroken.

Perhaps the most extraordinary test of all remains to be described. Two stout wooden rings were obtained, one made of alder, and the other of oak. They were several inches in diameter. These rings were strung on a band of catgut, together with an endless band of gut, and the ends of the first-mentioned band brought together on a sealed card, as in the other string experiments. Presently a rattling was heard under the one-legged round table, while a smell of something burning was perceived. On examination the two wooden rings were found encircling the leg of the round table, where they could not have been placed by any man without first removing the top or the feet, and the endless gut band was twined and knotted with the looped gut string. The odor was explained by the spirits writing on the customary slate that they could not further tie the endless band without burning it through. A white spot was found upon it, and similar ones appeared when the gut was held in or near a flame.

One other test deserves attention. Zollner had taken a round collar box and placed a coin therein. The box was then sealed up by pasting paper round the entire circumference, covering the juncture of the box and lid. In a little flat box he placed two pennies, and pasted it up in a similar manner. He did not look at the dates of these coins at all, and after awhile forgot the demomination of the largest. During the progress of the various tests, the boxes were forgotten, and it was not until Slade returned to Leipsic, six months afterwards, that Zollner found them, and brought them to the room. By shaking the round box he became satisfied that it contained a silver piece, but that was all. The boxes were lying on the table in full view, when Slade declared he saw "fünf, 1876." No one could make out what this

Plate 14. TABLE AND WOODEN RINGS.

meant, till Slade held a slate under the table, and with a clang the larger coin fell on the slate, when its denomination was seen by all to be *fünf*, or five, and its date 1876. On taking up the round box it was found to be empty, although the sealing was undisturbed.

Presently writing was obtained on the slate held under the table upon which this time two bits of pencil had been placed. The writing was, "10 Pfennig, 1876," "2 Pfennig, 1875." In a few moments two distinct sounds were heard on the slate, and upon withdrawing it there were the two coins of the denominations and dates just written, which dates, remember, no one present ever had known. The little box was then picked up from the table; but to the surprise of all a rattling sound was heard when it was shaken. Slade asked his spirits what caused this sound, when the answer was written on the slate, "The pencils are in the box." Everyone had forgotten the two bits of pencil which had been laid on the slate at the beginning of the test, but on opening the small box there they were found, while the seals showed no sign of rupture. These boxes and coins were photographed soon after.

Before concluding this sketch, I will mention that Dr. Nicolaus Wagner, professor of zoology at St. Petersburg, has carefully related how he and some friends witnessed a successful experiment with a book-slate lined with sooted paper, and then bound and sealed. No regular medium was present at all, but only their own party. After the slates had been tied for some time, they were opened, and nothing found. They were then sealed the second time, and after a while, on opening, the print of a hand was found on one side, and the print of a foot on the other. The hand print was shown to an artist friend, and immediately identified by him with that of a lady, who had previously formed one of their number, but had died. It is not stated whether the artist was a Spiritualist or not.

Some years ago the well-known Dr. Robert Hare was professor of chemistry at the University of Pennsylvania. Mr. S. A. Peters took to the laboratory two hermetically sealed glass tubes, and two small pieces of platinum. These were placed in a box, and the box laid upon the table in the presence of Dr. Hare and a medium. After some fifty minutes, the message came for Mr. Peters to open the box. He accordingly broke the seals and found the bits of platinum within the glass tubes.

A Dr. Nichols of London published, in 1878, that on April 7th of that year he carefully drew the ends of a strong cord through a hole in a card, and then sealed and stamped the whole. Immediately, in the presence of five persons, five knots were tied in the unbroken string. On the 19th he declared that he joined hands with Mr. Eglinton, and in a second a bent-wood chair was placed so as to hang on his arm, with his arm passing through the back, while his grip on his friend's hand had not been parted for a moment.

I have only mentioned these latter tests in order to show that a few other witnesses besides the German professor testify to equally mysterious occurrences.

Very recently Kellar, the famous *prestidigitateur*,

has written a remarkable article in one of the leading magazines, in which he describes some extraordinary feats of eastern jugglers, as witnessed by himself. He confesses his inability to account for them. On one occasion, in the presence of the Prince of Wales and some fifty thousand spectators, in Calcutta, in 1875, he saw a man laid on the points of three sharp swords, whose hilts were buried in the ground. He did not tip over, and the points of the swords did not penetrate his flesh. The old fakir then dug the soil away from and removed one sword, then the second, and the third, when the extended man lay as before, at the same height above the ground, and entirely unsupported. This was in broad daylight. Kellar afterwards satisfied himself of the sharpness of the swords.

He declares that he saw a conjuror in Zululand wave a bunch of grass over the body of a young man whom he had caused to lie upon the ground, when the grass took fire, burned and crackled, while the form of the man rose from the ground, and followed the waving of the grass, and finally settled down again on the earth. A few passes from the hands of the conjuror, and the young Zulu leaped to his feet as if nothing had happened.

Shortly after the Zollner sittings, Slade gave several seances in Bohemia at the house of a wealthy manufacturer named Schmid. From that place a report nearly as marvelous was given. There was a great amount of writing on slates which Slade had never seen before they were put in his hands. Two magnetic compasses were placed, one above the other, and Slade's hand passed over them. They were both affected, but oppositely, one turning one way, and the other in the reverse direction. Slade stood in the middle of the room, and Schmid and another near him. Schmid started to go into the next room when a large stone fell, as if from the air, on the floor at his feet with such violence as to make a hole in the floor; and immediately another fell in like manner.

Later, at Berlin, a slate was written on in six different languages. It was found to be free from chemical preparations; Slade had never seen it before the seance, and "there was not the smallest opportunity for effecting an exchange." Slade never touched it except to lay a bit of pencil between, and two unbelievers held it in full light while the writing took place.

On the other hand, when Slade appeared before the Henry Seybert Commission, at the University of Pennsylvania in 1885, he told those gentlemen that Zollner watched him closely during three or four sittings, but that after that he was allowed to do as he pleased. He told the commission that the spirits had forbidden him to use sealed slates any more. He showed the most barefaced assurance in attempting to palm off upon them the most ridiculously simple tricks of sleight of hand. When asked about Kellar, the *prestidigitateur*, and his tricks of slate and table, he said Kellar is a powerful medium.

Rev. Howard Furness, one of the commission, tells how he entertained Slade at his home on several occasions. He states that the last time he saw Slade he was in Boston. Dr. Furness inquired, " Well, and how are the old spirits coming on?" Slade laughed, and replied, " Oh pshaw!

You never believed in them, did you?" This was in April, 1887.

The commission secured several sittings from Professor Kellar, the magician. It is the united testimony of those engaged that his results " far surpassed anything done by Slade." A perfectly clean slate was placed beneath the edge of the table, with a part of the slate in view, and held in that position by the fingers of Kellar's right hand, his thumb being on top of the table. The observers watched most closely, and the thumb never moved, yet in a few minutes the slate was found covered with writing on both sides, and in seven languages. Kellar privately explained to one of the commission just how this was done.

Professor George Fullerton reports, after a visit to Leipsic, that Professor Fechner was nearly blind, and believed the tests because of his faith in Zollner. Professor Scheiber also had defective vision, and was not satisfied in his own mind as to the accuracy of their observations, while Weber, now of advanced age, had not recognized the disabilities of his fellows.

In concluding this chapter I refer to my own sittings with Slade, and the positive trickery he then offered as the work of spirits. Of course when such repeated evidence of fraud is brought forward against a medium, it is not possible to put faith in any reported manifestations in which he has been engaged. John W. Truesdell, in his "Bottom Facts of Spiritualism," narrates his experiences with Slade, which serve to still further reveal fraud and trickery. The scientific investigator desires to be open to the truth, but certainly this mine does not "pan out" enough to encourage further search.

Plate 15.   Chains of Darkness.

CHAPTER V.

The Latest Phenomena

AFTER some sixteen years have elapsed since the phenomena at Leipsic, the scientific world is again startled by the report of experiments conducted by eminent men, this time at Milan, Italy. The famous astronomer, Professor Schiapparelli, the discoverer of the canals on Mars, Professor Lombroso, of Turin, Professor Brofferio, who recently took the ten thousand franc prize for the best scientific article, Professor Richet, and others formed the investigating committee.

The sittings were held in Milan during September, 1892. The medium is Eusapia Paladino, from Naples. She is married, and is of robust appearance. Her husband is a carpenter, and she an ironer. She discovered her strange power when quite young, but took an aversion to it, and was only induced to give serious attention to the phenomena by the influence of Signor Ercolo Chiajia, a Neapolitan gentleman, distinguished by the king, and possessed of wealth. His avowed object was to bring her to the attention of scientific men. She never was accustomed to give public sittings.

During the progress of the experiments an editor offered to bet three thousand francs that he could explain all the tricks of the medium. To this she returned no answer, but Professor Aksakow, one of the committee, answered for her, and requested the editor to show the truth of the matter. The latter attempted to explain the effects produced by supposing the medium to shift her feet and hands in such a way as to fool the committee, and his explanation was generally accepted by the public, while the committee went right on with the experiments. Let it be noticed that the majority of the committee were not Spiritualists, and only Professor Schiapparelli had any theory in the case, his being derived from his old friend

Zollner, the astronomer of Leipsic, with whom we are already familiar.

One day another editor happened to meet Eusapia in the street and asked her to walk home with him, as his wife wanted to see her. Eusapia went. At the editor's house the kitchen table was brought in, and the members of the family seated themselves about it. The table immediately arose from the floor about six inches and remained suspended in the air for several seconds. It was about four o'clock in the afternoon, and the windows were open. Eusapia asked that they might be shut and this was done, but light remained sufficient to enable all to see. The usual phenomena occurred, moving of furniture, noises, appearance of hands, and so on. The editor next day took up the defense in his paper, pointing out the fact that all these things happened in a strange house, to which she had never been before, and where she certainly had no accomplice. Her coming was totally unexpected, and none of the party were Spiritualists.

Although this editor was well known, public

opinion was against the whole thing,* and many pronounced it against the decorum of the city. The mayor attended one of the sittings, which were held at the house of Signor Finzi, in a palace on the Via Monte de Pieta. The mayor said he felt a large, damp, hairy hand pass over his face, which was certainly not the hand of Eusapia.

Professor Schiapparelli was asked if he believed in the phenomena. His reply was, "How can I believe in a thing for which I can account in no way? I should define the phenomena as mediumistic, and I consider them of the greatest value to science." The committee reported partly as follows:—

"In consideration of the evidence given by Professor Cesare Lombroso regarding the mediumistic phenomena produced by means of Signora Eusapia Paladino, the undersigned met her at Milan to hold with her a series of experiments for the purpose of verifying such phenomena, submitting her to as rigorous observation as possible. We held in all seventeen sittings, which took

* Slade was expelled from Vienna by the public and the police in 1878.

place in the house of Signor Finzi, Via Monte de Pieta, between the hours of nine and twelve in the evening."

"The medium, who was invited to come to these sittings by Signor Aksakow, was presented by Cav. Chiajia, who was present at only a third of the sittings, and generally at the first and least important part of them."

"On account of the agitation made by the press in announcing these sittings, and seeing the diverse opinions of the press concerning Signora Eusapia and Cav. Chiajia, it seems well to publish the following brief account of what we have seen and experienced."

Some of the most interesting experiments were performed with an ordinary pine table about four feet long, and weighing twenty pounds. Among the several movements of the table by which answers to questions were given, it was impossible not to observe especially the motion made during the raps. . . . . The medium sat with both sleeves rolled up above her elbows, and held out both feet, beating them together, while the table stood on two legs and offered considerable resistance to an attempt to push it down. The table was connected with an apparatus for measuring the pressure. Then all hands were placed on the table in such a position that they could only push down, and the wish expressed that the pressure should decrease. At once the dynamometer indicated some fifteen pounds decrease. Reversing the conditions and arranging the hands so that they could only diminish the pressure, it increased about the same amount.

Again the table was entirely lifted from the floor, while only one hand of the medium rested on it; and in this position it was photographed several times. One leg of the table always touched the dress of the medium, but that was "insufficient to account for the phenomenon."

Similar to this was the "levitation" of the body of the medium. Being placed in a chair and suspended from a steelyard, her weight increased or diminished, as desired, to the extent of twenty-five to thirty-three pounds. When different members of the party attempted to force the scale to fluctuate beneath their weight they found it impossible beyond a very slight degree, no matter how violent their efforts. On another occasion the steelyard beat up and down violently when the dress of the medium was allowed to touch it, she being seated in a chair upon the floor. Professor Brofferio got down and held the dress, satisfying himself that there was no pressure communicated from it.

A chair a few yards away, in the full light, suddenly approached Professor Schiapparelli. He arose and put it back, when it approached him again.

Among the most important and significant facts they reckon the bodily elevation of the medium and her chair from the floor to the table, which took place upon September 28th and October 3d. The medium was seated at the end of the table, complaining loudly as if in pain, when she was lifted bodily upon the table with her chair, and placed in exactly the same position as before. During the whole of the time both her hands were held and accompanied by the hands of the gentlemen holding them. The chair was raised gently, and Sig. Richet and Professor Lombroso are sure they did not assist the lifting in the least. While others held her hands she was lifted down again and placed upon the floor.

On two occasions Professor Schiapparelli had his spectacles taken off in the dark, an operation requiring some care in the light on account of the delicate fastenings which he used to hold them on. But so gently was it done that he had to feel to be sure that they were gone. At another time he was struck and pounded, and many times hands were felt by different members of the committee and repeatedly seen by them all.

Schiapparelli was a friend of Professor Zollner, and the committee did not fail to try some of the famous tests recorded in his book; especially the wooden rings, the formation of a simple knot in an endless cord,* and the penetration of a solid object into a closed box But after repeated trials *not one of these succeeded.*

In concluding their report the committee state that at times they were not sure that they retained

* See pp. 97 and 107

Plate 16. THE PIT OF FIRE.

THE LATEST PHENOMENA. 129

both hands of the medium, so that grave doubts as to the appearing hands and the touches felt by them were possible, but concerning many of the tests they seem to be unanimously of the opinion that there was no trickery. They say:—

"In making public this brief and incomplete account of our experiences, we must again express our convictions that, in the circumstances given, none of the manifestations obtained in a more or less intense light, could have been produced by any artifice whatever; that the same conviction can be affirmed with regard to the greater part of those taking place in the darkness. For the rest, we recognize that from a strictly scientific point of view our experiments still leave very much to be desired. Nevertheless, they prove enough in our eyes to show that these phenomena are well worth scientific attention." The report is signed by Giovanni Schiapparelli, director of the observatory, Milan; Carl Du Prel, doctor of philosophy, Munich; Angelo Brofferio, professor of physics, Royal School of Agriculture; G. B. Ermacora, and Georgio Finzi, Ph. D. There were present sometimes Charles Richet, editor of the *Revue Scientifique* and Cesare Lombroso, M. D., of Turin.

Having frankly stated this on its merits, I now again call attention to the fact of the thorough investigation made in Philadelphia by the famous Seybert commission, a full report of which has been long published. This commission managed to bring before them the famous Dr. Slade very near the time of his sittings with the writer, as recorded in a previous chapter. In every respect he failed to do for them anything more than he did for me, and they detected him again in the most glaring frauds and tricks. Dr. Slade has been exposed again and again. He has passed the night with an investigator and been detected in a series of wild attempts to produce an impression of the supernatural upon his bedfellow. In all the years since the Zollner seances he has utterly failed to reproduce the famous tests recorded in that scientist's writings, and moreover, the most serious doubts as to Zollner's sanity are forced upon the investigator who follows the Seybert

THE LATEST PHENOMENA. 131

commission in their labors, and reads the report of Professor George Fullerton. All three of the surviving professors agreed that Zollner had a special theory of a fourth dimension which he was laboring to prove, and that his insanity, which developed later, was then really beginning, or probably so. Professor Fullerton questioned them carefully, but positively obtained nothing upon which to build up any real faith in the remarkable book of Professor Zollner.

Putting all these things together, it will be seen that unless the Milan performances stand the test of careful investigation better than those of Leipsic, there has really been nothing of any moment yet proven to show that spirits of any kind are able to produce important effects of the nature described and generally attempted by mediums. Of course, reports abound, like those of Colonel Olcott, who calmly relates how he held an egg in his hand, under a piano, and the lady of the house placing her hand beneath his, the whole side of the heavy piano rose in the air, supported upon the fragile egg. Thousands of such statements can be had for the asking; but the main point stands,—that not one of them has ever stood the test of calm, scientific investigation by those who had no axe to grind in the matter. All fade away, or at least become very hazy when closely examined. Trick seems to be ingrained in the whole thing from centre to circumference, and the wonder is that so many are fooled by the impositions.

'Even the jugglers themselves seem to be anything but bomb-proof against the deceits of the mediums. The court juggler in Zollner's book is an example. Professor Fullerton, of the University of Pennsylvania, in a letter to the writer, says that he did not see that gentleman while in Berlin, but adds: " Their testimony [jugglers] I regard as better than that of other people, but, of course, not as infallible. In two or three instances I have been rather surprised to find them inclined to ascribe to occult powers anything they were themselves unable to do. Possibly you have had the same experience."

Professor Zollner relates how Slade refused certain conditions suggested by some investigators, saying: "I claim to be honest and as earnest in this matter as those who call upon me for the purpose of investigation. Therefore I shall continue to object to all such worthless appliances whenever they are proposed." In the light of such exposures of his "honesty" as those given in this book, and in the admirable and amusing little work called "Bottom Facts of Spiritualism," such language by the redoubtable doctor cannot but excite a smile.

The words of Joel Tiffany may be repeated here: "I want to call your attention to the universal fact that, when a medium devoted to external manifestations is under the control of his presiding spirit, he is under an influence to deceive, to cheat, that is well-nigh irresistible." It may be that Professor Zollner in his haste to prove his pet theory, passed under the same kind of influence which the rest of us have found to be so strong in Dr. Slade. I merely offer this as a possible means of accounting for the extraordinary statements in his famous book, which if really true as recorded, would settle the matter of supernatural interference beyond question. To refer to Tiffany again, the breath seems to acquire the "odor of the onion-stalk through which it passes."

I think that the majority of sober thinkers who read the presentation I have given of both sides of this case will agree with me that the most favorable verdict possible so far for the claims of the Spiritists is the famous Scotch "not proven."

CHAPTER VI.

Spiritism—Its Inner Mysteries.

NOTWITHSTANDING all the frauds described in the foregoing chapter, there is very much more reality in Spiritism than most outsiders believe.

I am now about to speak in the plainest language of the deep iniquities of the thing, and to endeavor to sound a note of warning that may reach and save many from its appalling influence. These inner mysteries are as really true as the tricks and outer frauds with which the average person is fairly well acquainted. But the "mysteries" are not revealed in the first instance to the inquirer; they are held back until the neophyte has advanced to the proper state of mind for their reception.

Possession by spirits, or the residence in the human and animal body of beings of another order *is true, if the Bible is true.* The serpent in Eden possessed by Satan himself, was a tremendous fact, although the devil has labored most diligently to persuade men to disbelieve that story. Later, just before the flood, the fallen angels (called "sons of God" in the English version) took possession of the women of the time so thoroughly as to cause them to bear giant offspring, whose mighty sins were the crowning manifestation of evil in that wicked age. In the time of Moses the magicians of Egypt, headed by Jannes and Jambres, performed their miracles, even producing frogs and blood, as Moses did. It will not do for the reader to hastily conclude that they merely practiced sleight of hand, for the record distinctly says that "they did so with their enchantments." When the miracle of the lice was reached they were unable to reproduce it, or any subsequent miracle that Moses wrought at God's bidding. That they did possess some supernatural power is plain *if the Scriptures are true.* Still later we read of the Witch

Plate 17.   THE MESSENGER OF EVIL.

of Endor who "had a familiar spirit." Passing over into the New Testament we find the record of Simon the sorcerer, and of Elymas, and the distinct declaration that the oracular maid of Philippi was "possessed by a spirit of Python." (See margin. Python was the Old Serpent, and we see here the plainest statement of spirit control.) Acts xvi. 16.

Only a moment is necessary in which to prove that these spirits were not the souls of departed human beings. David said, when his baby died, "I shall go to him, but he shall not return to me." The parable of Lazarus and Dives plainly declares that "there is a great gulf *fixed*," so that none can pass either way.* If Jesus Christ is final authority on this point, then the last reference settles the question. The real truth is that the delusion of the Spiritists, that the departed friends revisit them, is specially of the devil. And in the endeavor to throw men off the right track, he diligently strives to make them believe that the spirits

---

* For the scientific law involved in the "great gulf," see "Alpha and Omega" in the chapter on "The Science of Sheol."

are anything but what they are, viz., the demons that wait on his bidding. It is the fashion now to disbelieve in a personal devil. But take care! As sure as you live, the next step is to doubt the existence of a *personal* God. The Bible is not one whit plainer on the personality of the one than the other. Look and see.

> Men don't believe in a devil now,
>   As their fathers used to do;
> They've forced the door of the broadest creed
>   To let his majesty through.
> There isn't a print of his cloven foot,
>   Or a fiery dart from his bow
> To be found in earth or air to-day,
>   For the world has voted so.
>
> But who is mixing the fatal draught
>   That palsies heart and brain,
> And loads the bier of each passing year
>   With ten hundred thousand slain?
> Who blights the bloom of the land to-day
>   With the fiery breath of hell,
> If the devil isn't, and never was,
>   Won't somebody rise and tell?
>
> Who dogs the steps of the toiling saint,
>   And digs the pit for his feet?
> Who sows the tares in the fields of time
>   Wherever God sows His wheat?

The devil is voted not to be,
  And of course the thing is true;
But who is doing the kind of work
  The devil alone should do?

We are told he does not go about
  Like a roaring lion now;
But whom shall we hold responsible
  For the everlasting row
To be heard in home, in church, in state,
  To the earth's remotest bound,
If the devil, by a unanimous vote,
  Is nowhere to be found?

Won't somebody step to the front forthwith,
  And make his bow, and show
How the frauds and crimes of a single day
  Spring up? We want to know;
The devil was fairly voted out,
  And of course the devil's gone,
But simple people would like to know
  Who carries his business on?

There is a devil, and there are demons, or the word of the Lord is of no possible account, for it does not mean what it says. And the special danger of the age is that the disguised modern "demon" be taken for what he purports to be — "an angel of light."

Are you aware that the seven nations of Canaan were Spiritists of the most pronounced type? No. A great many readers of the Bible are totally ignorant of this fact; and of course they do not know that God ordered their extermination *for this very reason;* but it is the exact truth. Read the record:—

"When thou art come into the land . . . . there shall not be found among you anyone that maketh his son or daughter to pass through the fire, or that useth divination, or an observer of times [*look out here for modern astrologists*], or an enchanter, or a witch, or a charmer, or a consulter with *familiar spirits,* or a wizard, or a necromancer. For all that do these things are an abomination unto the Lord; and, *because of these abominations,* the Lord thy God doth drive them out from before thee. Thou shalt be perfect with the Lord thy God. For these nations which thou shalt possess hearkened to observers of times, and unto diviners, but as for thee, the Lord thy God hath not suffered thee so to do." Deuteronomy, xviii. 9–14.

In another place, it is expressly stated that the

Canaanites "sacrificed unto demons." So this matter is placed beyond dispute, unless we object to the Bible.

Paul told the men of Athens that they were, "too much given to the worship of demons." Acts xvii. 22. This is the correct rendering according to Newton, Clark, Campbell, Wesley, and Doddridge, besides the Syriac and the Diaglott. He also told the Corinthians that all heathen worship was the worship of demons. "I say unto you, that the things that the Gentiles sacrifice, they sacrifice unto demons, and not to God." I. Corinthians, xix. 21. And looking down the ages, he warns the church to beware lest anyone "beguile you into a voluntary humility [*the laying down of the will, as is cardinally insisted upon in becoming a medium*] and worshipping of demons [*angels may be either good or bad; the word has no intrinsic good*], intruding into those things that he hath not seen, vainly puffed up in his fleshly mind." Colossians ii. 18.

That Satan specially desires to be worshipped is proved by his final temptation to Jesus: "All these things will I give thee if thou wilt fall down and worship me." To be in the place of God is his crowning ambition, and the very thing that his last great incarnation of evil, the "Man of Sin," will also essay to do. And that Spiritism is closely akin to these manifestations of the devilish is plain from the prayers offered to Satan himself. At San Jose, California, in January, 1874, Professor Chaney, in the opening of a debate with Elder Grant, publicly delivered the following prayer to Satan:—

"O, Devil, prince of demons in the Christian hell! O, thou monarch of the bottomless pit! thou king of scorpions having stings in their tails, to whom it is given to hurt the earth for five months, I beseech thee to hear my prayer. Thou seest the terrible strait in which I am placed, matched in debate with one of the big guns of Christianity. Remember, O prince of brimstone, that when thou stretchest out thine arm, the Christian's God cannot stand before thee for a moment. Therefore, we beseech thee to stand by us on this occasion. Bless thy servant in his labors before thee. Fill his mouth with words of wisdom. Enable him to defend thee from the false charges about to be made against thy Sulphurous Majesty, and triumph by truth and logic over his opponent, so that this audience may realize that thou art a prayer-hearing and a prayer-answering devil."

Lizzie Doten, in the Spiritist paper, the *Banner of Light*, prays as follows: "O, Lucifer! thou son of the morning, who fell from thy high estate, and whom mortals are prone to call the embodiment of evil, we lift our voices to thee. From the depths of thine infamy streams forth divine truth. As thou hast been the star of the morning, thou wilt again become an angel of light." Is II. Corinthians xi. 13, a special prediction of this devilment? There Paul wrote: "For Satan himself is transformed into an angel of light."

Still another, in the same journal, prayed: "O, thou prince of darkness and king of light; we ask and demand that we may know thee, for to know thee is to know more of ourselves. [*What unconscious truth that is!*] The church and the world tell us that the devil goeth about as a roaring lion, seeking whom he may devour; but we know thee as God's vicegerent, to stand at his left hand, the regenerator of mankind, the means of bringing up all things, intellectually and morally, to perfection." For much more on this subject I refer the reader to a book called "Demonology," by E. F. Hanson, Belfast, Maine.

To the Christian in search of evidence as to the reality of Spiritism, I say, read your Bible. Turn to II. Kings xix., and read of Mannasseh and his iniquities in this line. *These declarations of the Scripture are not foolishness.* God never pronounced such awful sentence upon a man for a mere idiotic superstition. Our wholesale rejection of these things puts our God in the position of one who furiously punishes people for thinking that the moon is made of green cheese. Is it not perfectly plain that God never issued such thunderous declarations against a mere folly and sham, with nothing real about it? This ought to be final *for the Christian.* Read of Ahab's lying prophet in Kings and Chronicles, twice related in all its

Plate 18. Drawing Nearer.

detail.* A dramatic picture, truly, fit to rank with that wonderful sixteenth chapter of Numbers.

The great God, seated on his throne, his angels about him, and "all the host of heaven" standing near. This last expression is, I think, always used in the Old Testament of the *demon* hosts. God calls for a volunteer to deceive Ahab, that he may go up and fall at Ramoth Gilead. Forth from the evil throng steps a *spirit,* saying, "I will go." And the question is asked, "How?" To which the spirit replies, "I will be a lying spirit in the mouths of his prophets." "Go," answers the Almighty, "and you shall succeed."

Certainly this is an extraordinary narration, and it cannot possibly be eliminated from the record. God has seen to it that it is told twice over in every word and detail in two different books. It is there, and it means exactly what it says. The evil spirits, always ready to do evil, as in the case of Job, receive *permission* to practice their deviltry. God does not directly send; he "shaves with a razor that is hired."† It plainly declares that these evil

* I. Kings xxii; II. Chronicles xviii. †Isaiah vii. 20.

spirits (*not dead people*) can thus enter into evil men, and cause them to speak words of false import, calculated to deceive. God's justice sees to it that the real prophet appears, and warns Ahab of the danger, but he willfully turns away, and is destroyed.

Isaiah speaks of the people who seek unto "spirits that peep and mutter," and warns against the "living seeking to the dead."* Jeremiah writes in similar terms; and everywhere we read of "familiar spirits." Daniel read the writing on the wall, which was unintelligible to the master Spiritists of the time. They could read the writing of *their master*, but not of Daniel's God. The true religion stopped their mouths and destroyed their power, just as it has always done. True, indeed, is the admission of their own writers, already quoted, that Christianity has always been the foe of Spiritism. The two are exact opposites. One goeth up and the other down. *And one is as really a fact as the other.* Do not forget that.

All Christians believe the accounts of spirit

* viii. 19.

"possession" recorded in the New Testament. Spiritists have sought to prove the reappearance of friends from these cases. But they forget that the Jews always considered those persons to be under the power of demons. Tertullian challenges the enemy to admit that the Christians forced the oracles to confess that they were under the devil's influence. In modern times, such able medical authorities as Forbes Winslow, of England, declare that the demoniac is readily distinguished from the ordinary lunatic by a "strange duality," which the expert soon learns to recognize. They always consider such cases the most incurable. The boy at the foot of the mount (Mark ix. 26) is no more distinctly branded with the demon power than a host of modern cases, a few of which I have met with.

The Gadarene swine offer a singular illustration of this possession. A "legion" was about six thousand. All these demons had been abiding in one poor wretch of a man, but when distributed among two thousand swine the whole herd at once committed suicide. It appears that three demons was more than any hog would stand, while one man had lived with six thousand. Certainly fallen man is worse than any brute.

Recent cases of spirit possession can be given by the score. I refer to the New Year's number (1892) of *The Review of Reviews* for a very large collection of facts on this point. Another case I will give in some detail. A few years ago, in a New England town, lived a family of Spiritists, among whom was a young girl who greatly desired to be a Christian. After a while she became "possessed," and manifested all the strange and terrible symptoms described in the Bible. She would be suddenly thrown on the floor in the most frantic convulsions, exposing herself unless forcibly held down, and speaking profane and horribly obscene words in a strong voice, not at all her own. A dear friend of mine*—an old man simple and true in his faith, was called in to pray over her, the doctors all declaring that they could do nothing at all. He began to command the spirits to come out of her, in the name of Jesus Christ. The

* Ethan Allen, of Springfield, Mass.

voice would answer him, and strive to engage him in argument; but he kept steadily on, and refused any sort of compromise. (In the midst of the most frightful language he would command the demons, in Jesus' name, to hold their tongues; and they would be forced to obey.) After a time the paroxysm would pass, and the girl become as rational as ever, and have no knowledge of what she had uttered. This state of things continued for several weeks, towards the close of which the voice perceptibly weakened, and the demon complained that four of his brothers had left him, and that he would have to go out very soon. In a whining, whimpering voice he said, "I suppose I will have to go out. I wouldn't do it if I did not have to." When my friend mentioned the name of Jesus, her face would be twisted into the most horrible appearance, and the voice cried out, "Jesus! (I hate Jesus. You love him and He loves you; but I hate him." Finally she was delivered, and at last accounts was married and living happily with her family. I could give others just as marked. These things are not trumpeted abroad. The families of people so affected are not likely to court newspaper interviews, but strive to bury the thing out of sight and knowledge. But those who have been on the inside know that these things are true.

When the Apostle declared that "We wrestle not against flesh and blood, but against spirits of wickedness in the heavenlies," Ephesians vi. 12, he meant exactly what he said. It was no figure of speech. It is the purpose of this little book to sound a warning cry in these "last days" to arouse the people of God to a knowledge of the *real* nature of our adversaries. If the Scripture be true *we are standing on the eve of the greatest iniquity the world has ever known, and at such a time, to depreciate the power of the enemy is worse than foolish; it is suicidal.*

This state of things is most distinctly foretold in the Word. "The Spirit speaketh expressly, that in the latter times some shall depart from the faith, giving heed to *seducing spirits* and doctrines of demons; forbidding to marry," etc. I. Timothy iv. In Revelation xvi. 13, 14, we read of the "three unclean spirits, like frogs," which are "the spirits of demons, working miracles," etc. And Paul speaks to Timothy of the men who "creep into houses and lead captive silly women, laden with sins, led away with divers lusts; ever learning and never able to come to the knowledge of the truth." II. Timothy iii. 6.

These passages are closely descriptive of the peculiar heresies of this day, when so much is said of "deep things" and "higher knowledge." The women are strangely prominent in all these esoteric theories and teachings, and are plainly exemplifying the words of the Apostle just quoted. The sex question is wonderfully mixed up in the Spiritisms of the time, and it means much more than most people are aware. Dr. Cyrus Teed, of Cincinnati, Prince Michael, of Detroit, Schwinefurth, of Rockford, Illinois, and many others of the false Christs and eccentric "Esoterics" and "Theosophs" are fair examples of the fulfillment of these scriptures. All "lead captive silly women"; and with most of them as with the "Agapemone," and with "King Solomon," "*nee* John Wood," in England, the gravest charges of positive immorality have been freely made, with much color of truth in the evidence adduced. If Revelations ix. 20 be true for the latter times, men are to "worship demons" even in the closing days of this age, after all the boasted progress of nineteen centuries. Certain it is that the *deepest iniquity* of to-day lies along the line of *strange abuses of the sex principle in connection with the spirit world.*

In Mr. Stead's article, to which I have already freely alluded, he sums up what he calls "The seamy side of Spiritualism" in these words: "The phenomena of trance which are to be witnessed at the seance, when the medium professes to be taken possession of by any intelligence, are not such as to commend them to any prudent man or woman who has any respect for their individuality. When in the trance, as it is technically called, women who cannot bear the smell of tobacco will smoke a pipe as easily as the most inveterate smoker, and teetotallers will drink whisky as eagerly as habitual drunkards. In automatic

Plate 19. The Creation of Eve.

writing, which is one of the simplest forms of spiritualist manifestations, it is on record that young girls of unimpeachable character have been made the agent for producing writing, and drawing pictures, the very nature of which they were fortunately unable to understand. There is no necessity for going further into this subject beyond a general statement that at some seances, whether through self-hypnotism, or through the presence of invisible agencies, sitters have had experiences which may have been purely subjective, and have had no objective reality, but which are none the less degrading and abominable. To expose yourself to all the chances of such things may be justifiable, if out of the midst of all these temptations and suggestions to mental and moral disease you have a tolerable certainty of being able to gain some counterbalancing advantage. But, so far as I see, the chances for the ordinary man and woman are too slender. *[This tree of the knowledge of good and evil seems to bear so much more evil than good that Eve had better stay her hand.]**

* Italics mine. — *R. K. C.*

What stronger proof could possibly be found of the damning power of this sin than that in the statement recently made in an English journal, *Prophetic News and Israel's Watchman*, of the conversion to Spiritism of no less a personage than Mr. Stead himself. After reading the last paragraph such a thing seems impossible, but here is the statement from that journal, March, 1893. It is headed, " Mr. Stead Turned Spiritualist."

"Mr. W. T. Stead, who has obtained great notoriety as a writer and speaker during the past few years, was publicly withstood in February, last year (1892), at a meeting at Cardiff, by Alderman Richard Cory, J. P., who denounced Mr. Stead's strange, novel, and unorthodox teachings as subversive of the Gospel. This was related in the *Christian Herald* of February 25, 1892. Mr. Cory's penetration of Mr. Stead's heresies has been since abundantly justified by Mr. Stead's open advocacy of Spiritualism, and avowal of himself as a spiritualistic medium controlled by a familiar spirit whom he calls 'Julia.' Mr. Stead announces as a new and marvelous discovery that if he places his right hand and arm motionless on the table, an invisible spirit assumes control of it and writes communications from the spirit world in a totally different handwriting from his own ordinary caligraphy. But, so far from being new, it has been done every day for more than forty years in America by writing mediums, who are as plentiful as blackberries there since Spiritualism first appeared in the Fox family in 1848, 1849. Dr. Nichols, the discoverer of the Food of Health, gave a fair and candid description of American Spiritualism in his 'Forty Years in America,' and we have quoted it on a subsequent page, as well as another writer's 'Strange Confessions of a Spiritualist.' Spiritualism is simply a modern revival of the ancient sorcery and witchcraft and dealing with familiar spirits, denounced in the Bible, and foretold to be revived in these latter times under the sixth vial in Revelation xvi. 13, 14, and II. Timothy iii."

After all Mr. Stead has written, after all his investigations, and his former conclusions as to fraud and evil in the matter, this conversion seems most unaccountable. Truly, it serves to fearfully emphasize his words of warning just quoted on a previous page. So incredible did it appear to me, that I at once wrote to him direct, telling him of my intention of issuing a book on this subject, and asking him if this statement is true, as I did not wish to misrepresent him or any man. But no reply has reached me. I give it, therefore, on the authority of the journal mentioned, still hoping that it may be corrected in the future, or, at least, that the departure from the right path may not be so bad as reported.

A writer in the *North China Herald* tells of a visit paid to the poet Tennyson a few years ago. Lord Tennyson told of something that had happened in the room in which they were seated. "You see that table," he said, pointing to a huge, massive piece of furniture in the corner. Then he went on to tell how one night a trial was made at table turning, with the result that that very table raced about, and spun and turned and twisted and capered to such an extent that even those accustomed to such proceedings felt a certain consternation. **Suddenly the thing** stopped dead. The moment **before Bishop** Wilberforce **had** entered the room and mentally exclaimed, "(In the name **of God the Father, God the Son, and God the Holy Ghost, I adjure thee to be still."** The table never danced in the Bishop's presence again.

In this connection I feel bound to relate a somewhat similar experience of my own. I had given several lectures in the city of San Francisco, in the year 1892, among them two upon **Spiritualism.** At the close of one of them **I** was approached **by a little lady who desired** me to call at her house, stating that certain manifestations had been occurring there, from which **she** had derived some revenue, but about which she was now concerned. She said she was not a Spiritualist, and desired to know the truth. Taking a gentleman with me, **I called upon** her, and **was received** by herself and husband. A small table was produced and she proceeded to ask aloud if "they" would write and answer questions. Holding a pencil loosely in her hand the point described trembling and scrawling lines upon a sheet of paper which could be resolved into words with a little care. In this way she got answers. Putting her hands on the table it would tip three times to signify yes, and twice for no. With her husband's hands also upon it, the table behaved in the same way. I specially noticed that the motions of the table did not follow her fingers, but the fingers seemed to follow the table. I mean by this that when a person rests the tips of the fingers upon a table and endeavors to cause the same to tip or rock, the fingers will be seen to move forward slightly first and then the table moves. But in this case there was no such motion visible. I am perfectly familiar with the possible methods of invisible black threads attached to the table, as well as with the use of finger rings with sharp projecting points or claws. Neither of these were used. She protested that she did not will to move the table at all, and that she was not conscious of the least effort to do so.

The phenomenon, however, was so insignificant, and so many requests for variations failed to bring forth anything, that I could not feel very much

SPIRITISM—ITS INNER MYSTERIES. 165

impressed. I then placed my hands on the table with the lady, mentally commanding any possible "spirits" in the name of Jesus Christ to let it alone. She asked for many things, but except a slight struggling effort, no motion whatever occurred. She reproached the "spirits," and accused them of promising a good sitting and then going back on the promise, but all to no effect. Taking up her pencil she asked for reasons for this action. Presently the scrawling writing replied: "I am afraid." On getting this she eagerly pressed for an explanation, and asked of what or of whom they were afraid. The answer was written: "Seen cloud over man."

This was all that occurred, and I was compelled to tell her that while I regarded the tests as extremely inconclusive, yet whatever might be of a supernatural character, if any of it, must certainly be set down as evil, and only evil. She seemed impressed, and promised to abandon the practice. What looked strange to her was that these "spirits" had told her to go to a religious meeting and try to save souls, and that she had been enabled to pay off her husband's debts from the money paid her by persons desiring sittings. She could not see how evil spirits could advise good actions or do any good.

I said: "Did you ever go a-fishing?"

"Oh, yes, often."

"Did you fish with bait, or did you use a bare hook?"

"I fished with bait, of course."

"Was the bait something through which the fish could see the hook, something they did not like, or was it what they specially preferred?"

"Of course it was something they liked."

"Well, do you not see that if you are to be caught by the hook of Spiritism, the bait must be something that attracts you?"

She said she saw the fitness of the comparisons, and was no longer surprised at the course taken by her mysterious visitors

A most remarkable book, called the "Powers of the Air," has lately been published by a man who had been and now is a Christian, but who fell under the influence of Spiritism and became a medium of very high development. I make a few extracts from this book.

The voice said to him that he (the voice) was God himself, and that the medium had been chosen as a very special agent in the salvation of the race. He was promised that on a certain day the greatest revival ever known should break out, and many of his friends be converted. This prediction and several others failed, when the voice explained that evil men interfered. After a number of false predictions, including one that sent the man to New York on a wild-goose chase, he was convinced that the whole thing was a delusion. He then questioned the spirits at length as to their motives for such actions, and received some very extraordinary answers. They said:—

"You were forced into the belief that Spiritualism is but the harbinger of the millennial glory by the first communications. They were certainly grand, and were given you with the express intention of leading you to believe they were from Jesus Christ and God himself. You ought to have suspected this. All hooks are baited with a very gilded bait."

Question: "Are not the doctrines taught generally by the Spiritualists denominated in Scripture the doctrines of devils or demons?"

Answer: "Yes; they are in very deed the doctrines of demons, because they generally reject the teaching of Jesus Christ and his apostles and followers. A. J. Davis was inspired to my certain knowledge by the prince of demons, or, in other words, the most intellectual demon belonging to the powers of the air. His 'Harmonial Philosophy' was all written under inspiration of demon influence. There is no Jesus Christ, nor any doctrine taught by Jesus Christ in his works; they are all Christless or Anti-Christ. . . . . Spiritualism was conceived in sin and brought forth in iniquity. It is a dead carcass, a carcass that will be a stench to the good of the whole earth."

Q. "But do you not expect it to be better?"

A. "Never. We are the debris of God's moral creation, cast off as far as we know, only to be destroyed."

Q. "But do not the pious dead surround those

who are still in the body, as guardians from the evil influence?"

A. "They are never seen by us if they do. We see nothing around the pious any more than around the wicked. But we are often around them ourselves, infusing into their minds some infidel or atheistic thought, to see how they will receive it. We take delight in disturbing and irritating them, just as we do you."

Q. "Do you not think that good spirits develop mediums, and communicate through them as you do?"

A. "I think not. We think we are warranted in the conclusion that no pious dead, nor the spirits of just men made perfect, nor angels, have anything to do with controlling mediums at the present day."

"These spirit manifestations are clearly prophesied of by the apostle Paul in II. Thessallonians: 'And then shall that wicked be revealed, whom the Lord shall consume with the spirit of his mouth, and shall destroy with the brightness of his coming; even him whose coming is after the working of Satan, with all power and signs and lying wonders, and with all deceivableness of unrighteousness in them that perish; because they received not the love of the truth, that they might be saved. And for this cause God shall send them strong delusion, that they should believe a lie; that they might be damned who believed not the truth, but had pleasure in unrighteousness.' This passage sets forth the signs of these times so clearly that all the righteous or pious can understand."

"We have been provoked to reveal to you the fact that all the revelations through mediums, to the effect that all men are progressing to a state of holiness and happiness are false, totally and absolutely false.* We have as good an opportunity to know the facts connected with all the modern revelations as any spirit can know in the world, and we certainly know they are not from God, but from spirits, some of them guilty of greater abuses, if it were possible, than we have inflicted upon you."

"You ask how we know that modern spiritual-

* The optimists who eloquently preach of how the world is getting better, should make a note of this. — *R. K. C.*

Plate 20. Innocence.

istic demonstrations are not from God? We answer that they are made by spirits who hate God, and have no fellowship with that which is good. (They universally reject the Bible as the Word of God, denouncing it as false and unworthy of belief.) All the revelations yet made by spirit manifestations have not so much of the Gospel truth in them as has yet resulted in the regeneration of one soul, in the sense that Jesus Christ taught regeneration. The revelations of these spirits are just what you might expect from beings who have not the love of God in them."

This gentleman, who had also been used as a medium, also asked the question: "To what extent have the powers of the air dominion and rule over the children of men?"

A. "They have the power to produce lifelike images in the minds of irrepressible mediums. This is often understood by them to be an actual sight of a real object. This leads to a great variety of delusions. Those who are called the leaders of Spiritualism, and who know the fallacy of these impressions, allow the deception to go on, and are therefore participators in the swindle. This stamps them with infamy. The spirits have the power of *using the human body with all its organs and faculties.** This is done in the case of trance speakers and personating mediums. They enter the body by means of electrical and galvanic influences, and having entered, use the vocal organs. They also possess the power to move ponderable objects, such as chairs and tables. This is generally accomplished by the agency of scores and hundreds of the invisible workers."

The author says: "They could imitate the manner of speech peculiar to my relatives and acquaintances, and so exactly did they give the inflections and intonations of their voices that I would have been compelled to believe the imitations to be real had they not personified some whom I knew to be living."

"That the reader may be fortified at every point, and never be drawn into the belief that any communication from the spirit world can in any sense be from God (though it breathes the very

* Italics mine. — *R. K. C.*

spirit of heaven itself, and be characterized by lofty sentiment, and the most elegant phraseology, and classic purity of style), let him remember that if such are given through yourself as a medium, it will be only the prelude to something monstrous and absurd. (All my experiences of these beings who surround us in the air, sum up this distinct conclusion; that they delight in evil as their chief object, and especially that branch of evil called deception.) If any one thing pleases them more than any other, it is to make those in the earth life believe the most monstrous and absurd theories. I would exhort the reader, as did the Apostle Paul, 'Though we, or an angel from heaven, preach any other gospel unto you, let him be accursed.'"

"The most subtle method which these powers of the air use to induce belief in their monstrous absurdities, consists in making friendly allusions to Jesus Christ and his gospel, and in speaking very highly of some of its doctrines, and perhaps giving a grand dissertation upon one of them, and in the meantime *weave into the framework of this dissertation a subtle philosophy which would undermine the consistency of the whole and render it perfectly delusive."*

Of course, the skeptic will object that all these "confessions" were simply the work of a disordered imagination in the mind of the converted medium. But I am not writing so much for the skeptic as for those who have put together some of the overwhelming evidences of the pernicious nature of Spiritism in any and all of its forms, and who may be warned in time of the certain results that come from placing the least confidence in its integrity. Of course, these confessions are in full accord with the frank admissions of fraud made by leading Spiritualists themselves, which we have already quoted.

As to the tendency towards impurity and positive immorality, too much can scarcely be said. I have already given some very damaging statements on this point, but there is much more to be given. Perhaps the following from prominent advocates of Spiritism may be considered conclusive, in part at least.

Dr. Hatch, husband of Cora Richmond, who traveled for years in the interests of Spiritism, says: "The most damning iniquities are everywhere perpetrated in spiritualistic circles. . . . . It is worse than useless to talk to the Spiritualists against this condition of things; for those who occupy the highest position among them are aiding and abetting in all classes of iniquities that prevail among them. The abrogation of the marriage tie, bigamy accompanied by robbery, theft, rape, are all chargeable to Spiritualism. I most solemnly affirm that there has not arisen during the past five hundred years a people who are guilty of so great a variety of crimes and indecencies as the Spiritualists of America."

Dr. Potter says: "After years of careful investigation we are compelled to admit that more than one half of our traveling media, speakers, and prominent Spiritualists, are guilty of immoral and licentious practices that have justly provoked the abhorrence of all right-thinking people. Hundreds of families have been broken up, and many affectionate wives deserted by 'affinity' seeking husbands. Many once devoted wives have been seduced and left their husbands and tender helpless children to follow some 'higher attraction.'"

John M. Spear, a noted medium, in a lecture in Utica, New York, said: "Cursed be the marriage institution; cursed be the relation of husband and wife; cursed be all who sustain legal marriage." His "affinity" bore him an illegitimate child, and this is what she said about it in public: "I will exercise the dearest of all rights, the holiest and most sacred of all heaven's gifts, the right of maternity, in the way which to me seemeth right; and no man, or set of men, no church, no state, shall withhold me from the realization of that purest of all inspirations inherent in every true woman, the right to rebeget myself, when and by whom, and under what circumstances, seems to me fit and best." Modern Spiritualism, p. 147.

With such things as these before us shall we wonder at the prediction of Scripture that the strangest impurities shall mark the decline and fall of the last of earth's empires? And when we find all these strange delusions, all these so-called esoteric beliefs, with one accord opposing with might and main the central truths of the Divinity of Jesus, and the virtue of the Blood Atonement, shall we not open our eyes to the great fact that we live in an age that is peculiarly characterized by the word ANTICHRIST.

Finally I remind my readers of the words of Jesus, that the last days, preceding his second advent shall be days like to those of Noah and Lot; and when we recall that both those periods were marked by the strangest and most horrible uncleanness, is it altogether a matter of surprise that these things are really so? Without further delay I will pass to the consideration of the question, "What was the Tree of Knowledge?" Let even those who have closely followed me thus far prepare to be surprised at the revelations of demonism herein for the first time set forth in unvarnished language. Were it not that I am persuaded that the "Mystery of Iniquity doth already work," and that it is simply bound to have its swing, I would never dream of publishing these things. But God's word has declared that they shall be, and that they have been; and if God saw fit to speak of them, surely we cannot sit in judgment and condemn all utterance on the subject. The great fact is that we, "upon whom the ends of the world are come," are called upon to withstand "Spirits of wickedness in the heavenlies," who "have great wrath, knowing that the time is short;" and we cannot afford to shrink from the whole truth because it is horrible and disagreeable. Of course it is horrible to one who loves God. But that our friends may be saved from the horrible fate of being led astray into these unspeakably awful temptations, coming to them as "angels of light," I do not hesitate to tear aside the deceptive veils and show the real demons in all their native hideousness.

Do not too hastily pronounce these things to be evolved from the imagination of the writer. Before doing so, look carefully to the closeness of the logic and the remarkable thread of thought and statement in the Scriptures; then ask yourself the question: If the Bible be true, what other conclusion can be drawn? and if it be not true, how in the world did so many writers come to put down so many things which connect with one another and form a consistent whole?

PART SECOND.

The Original Sin.

CHAPTER 1.

The Sex Question.

AT the very beginning of this chapter I wish to warn my readers that this is not a dogmatic assertion of a wonderful discovery, but strictly what is called "A Study." Let this be borne in mind whenever the reader feels disposed to differ with the writer. I do not say that I do not believe it; I do believe that this study contains a very deep and a tremendously important truth for these last days. But I submit the evidence as logically as I can, and leave it with the reader on its inherent merits. As I have stated in the preface, the language will be perfectly plain in speaking of delicate matters; as plain as a lecture before a class in medicine. In giving this subject as a lecture I give it to men only, and to women only, just as the plainest medical lectures are given. In these days of agitation on the Social Purity question people are getting used to much more explicit descriptions of sexual matters than has been customary for a long time. And this, if properly conducted, is a good thing; we have too long neglected the most important points of vital interest to the race. In the earnest belief that this subject is of the greatest value to one who expects to be equipped for the war with the "spirits of wickedness in the heavenlies" in these last days, I consent to give these studies to my fellow men.

"Coming events cast their shadows before." A great many things are more or less current among us which really belong in their fullness to the next age. All sorts of efforts are being made to forestall the Millennium, as that wondrous age draws near. Mankind is eagerly bending forward, looking for "The Coming Man," for the "Golden Age"; and a variety of schemes are constantly appearing, intended to bring about that age, and produce that man by human agencies. Edward

Plate 21.   Envy of Others' Peace.

Bellamy "Looks Backward" on a set of imaginary human operations which have brought about an age when greed and lust have taken a holiday, and unselfishness has become general. The so-called Christian Socialist is looking for the adoption of a set of measures that will insure the equal division of everything. The nominal church member talks, and the average popular preacher preaches, of the speedy conquest of the world by the church, as it now is. Every one, Christian, infidel, Mohammedan, heathen, high and low, bond and free, are looking for another age, when all things will be better. And as they look, they instinctively strive to hasten it by effort, and plan, and work. They cannot help this; it is an instinct in the race to do so under such circumstances.

To make a heaven on earth is the dream of fallen humanity. Every single soul of Adam's posterity has at one time in his life yielded more or less to this instinct, and striven to realize this dream. Cain's descendants began the long line of inventions and "arts" which have ever been the stream to which men resort in their desire to slake the burning thirst for happiness that is the secret spring of all the work and effort of humanity. Not that these sciences and arts are sinful in themselves; no, that is not it, but they are sought by the race in the blind effort to make this world a paradise *in spite of the curse of the law.*

In this unconscious groping after the light, the agency of the "Prince of this world" is very apparent. And, as men reach out for that which is promised in the future, he manages to get them to forestall the sins of the future. This is just what we might expect, for how can a fallen being ever reach the truth by his own efforts? If he looks for happiness, being entirely poisoned with sin, he naturally travels along the channels which sin has worn; and therefore, in striving to anticipate happiness, he only anticipates other and greater sins.

Whatever men may think or say, it is certain that nothing is becoming of more striking importance than the SEX question. A mighty impetus has been given to its discussion of late through the Social Purity movement already referred to.

The race has been so long given over to impurity that people have realized something must be done, if possible, to stem the terrible tide of sin and death sweeping over the world. Licentiousness has run riot, as it always has in an age of wealth and luxury. But the thinkers are aroused. Papers are published on this subject, and the discussion has been marked by a plain directness and calm technical consideration that has done much to remove a false modesty, and prepare men and women to know more about themselves and their children than they had dreamed to be of any importance, except to physicians.

As in all new movements, some of these advocates of purity are inclined to go to extremes. Several publications are stoutly maintaining that intercourse between the sexes should never take place except for the propagation of the race; while others go still further, and contend that the only way to secure the highest holiness is to be continent altogether. In other words, the asceticism which made the first monks and nuns is again coming to the front. Much truth is mixed up with error in these writings. An admirable sermon lately delivered by the Rev. Mr. Clymer has been taken up by Fowler and Wells, and issued in pamphlet form. The subject is "Food and Morals," and the writer forcibly argues for the legitimate effects of food on the moral nature, presenting an array of facts that are exceedingly profitable to any reader. Eat good food, and you will be on the high road to health and happiness. Fill your stomach with all sorts of indigestible and corrupting substances, and the quickest means are employed to bring about a general state of corruption in the moral nature. People are beginning to learn this fundamental principle, and the papers referred to make a great deal of it. But with the truth much error has crept in.

We are told that care in food and habits of life will radically change the nature. One writer talks of the race "being bred up to purity and the Millennium." Again he says: "The Millennium of purity, happiness, and intense chastity can never come except by cheerful obedience to prenatal laws." And another goes so far as to assert that by practicing **continence**, except for the propagation of offspring, the race will become pure, and "a generation of miniature Jesus Christs will be brought into being."

This is the same old, old error, the mistake of supposing effects can come before causes. It is looking for the consequent without the antecedent, for the kingdom without the king. Anticipating again. When will man learn to take the scientific plan?*

The visible effects of sin have been so terrible that there is no wonder men have restlessly sought for relief. On this question of sex such dreadful things have been brought to light by the investigations of the Social Purity agitators, by Mr. Stead, in the *Pall Mall Gazette* revelations, and by others, that people have been startled into attention to the subject as never before. Read the following, and then say whether it is not high time that even more is said and done to check the awful tide:—

* On this point see "Alpha **and Omega, or The** Birth and Death of the World," for a full discussion of the matter.

"To his Excellency, the Viceroy and Governor-General of India:—

"*May it please Your Excellency,* The undersigned ladies, practicing medicine in India, respectfully crave Your Excellency's attention to the following facts and considerations:—

"1. Your Excellency is aware that the present state of the Indian law permits marriages to be consummated not only before the wife is physically qualified for the duties of maternity, but before she is able to perform the duties of the conjugal relation, thus giving rise to numerous and great evils.

"2. This marriage practice has become the cause of gross immoralities and cruelties which, owing to existing legislation, come practically under the protection of the law. In some cases the law has permitted homicide and protected men who, under other circumstances, would have been criminally punished.

"3. The institution of child-marriage rests upon public sentiment, vitiated by degenerate religious customs and misinterpretation of religious books. There are thousands among the better educated classes who would rejoice if Government would take the initiative and make such a law as your memorialists plead for, and in the end the masses would be grateful for their deliverance from the galling yoke that has bound them to poverty, superstition, and the slavery of custom for centuries.

"4. The present system of child-marriage, in addition to the physical and moral effects which the Indian governments have deplored, produces sterility, and consequently becomes an excuse for the introduction of other child-wives in the family, thus becoming a justification for *polygamy*.

"5. This system panders to sensuality, lowers the standard of health and morals, degrades the race, and tends to perpetuate itself and all its attendant evils to all future generations.

"6. The lamentable case of the child-wife, Phulmani Dassi, of Calcutta, which has excited the sympathy and the righteous indignation of the Indian public, is only one of the many cases that are continually happening, the final results being quite as horrible, but sometimes less immediate. The following instances have come under the personal observation of one or another of Your Excellency's petitioners:—

"A. Aged nine. Day after marriage, left *femur* dislocated, *pelvis* crushed out of shape, flesh hanging in shreds.

"B. Aged ten. Unable to stand, bleeding profusely, flesh much lacerated.

"C. Aged nine. So completely ravished as to be almost beyond surgical repair. Her husband had two other living wives, and spoke very fine English.

"D. Aged ten. A very small child, and entirely undeveloped physically. This child was bleeding to death from the *rectum*. Her husband was a man of about forty years of age, weighing not less than eleven stone. He had accomplished his desire in an unnatural way.

"E. Aged about nine. Lower limbs completely paralyzed.

"F. Aged about twelve. Laceration of the *perineum* extending through the *sphincter ani*.

"G. Aged about ten. Very weak from loss of blood. Stated that great violence had been done her in an unnatural way.

"H. Aged about twelve. Pregnant, delivered by *craniotomy* with great difficulty on account of the immature state of the *pelvis* and maternal passage.

"I. Aged about seven. Living with husband. Died in great agony after three days.

"K. Aged about ten. Condition most pitiable. After one day in hospital was demanded by her husband, for his "lawful" use, he said.

"L. Aged eleven. From great violence done her person will be a cripple for life. No use of her lower extremities.

"M. Aged about ten. Crawled to hospital on her hands and knees. Has never been able to stand erect since her marriage.

"N. Aged nine. Dislocation of *pubic arch*, and unable to stand or put one foot before the other.

"In view of the above facts, the undersigned lady doctors and medical practitioners appeal to

Your Excellency's compassion to enact or introduce a measure by which the consummation of marriage will not be permitted before the wife has attained the full age of fourteen (14) years. The undersigned venture to trust that the terrible urgency of the matter will be accepted as an excuse for the interruption of Your Excellency's time and attention.

"Written and prepared by Mrs. N. Monelle-Mansell, M. A., M. D., Lucknow, India. Submitted to Government 22d September, 1890. Signed by fifty-five lady doctors. The above facts should elicit the compassion of all enlightened womanhood in behalf of child-wives. Are not they of more consequence than our dumb animals upon which we lavish so much sympathy and affection? N. M.-M."

Such horrors as these surely indicate that there is something wrong, something fundamental; but what can it be? If we ask of the brute creation, we at once notice a radical difference. Here no such sins take place. Instinct rules absolutely. Why such a difference in the human family, for

THE SEX QUESTION. 199

we are also animals? It is not sufficient to assign the presence of reason as the sole cause for such perversion, for the other appetites are not so much affected. The question is imperative now, when so many are teaching total abstinence. The Esoterics talk glibly of the "adepts," who are away beyond the pull of human passion, and who thereby are able to exert the most miraculous power over nature. The Rosicrucians of old are outdone by these latter-day saints of a new religion. The pedantic author of "Koreshanism" lately wrote in his paper of a time soon to come when by a "conflagration of males and females the real 'marriage of the lamb' will be brought about, for these [who are thus conflagrated] will be the first fruits of the kingdom." The Theosophs in grand conclave in Chicago, in 1892, told of the "Mahatmas," secluded in the fastnesses of Thibet, who are so marvelously powerful that if an ordinary mortal should happen to come into their presence, he would be incinerated immediately. (This explains why the general newspaper reporter has never been able to interview a Mahatma yet.) Those wonderful beings considerately seclude themselves from common view in order to save making so many piles of ashes of the unfortunates who might be tempted to break in and gaze; but remember, all this is soberly believed by multitudes of the educated elite of the land.

Is there any wonder that Paul wrote of the "seducing spirits" to whom men would give heed in the last times? They are surely here; but note this specially. In the midst of this strange tide of teaching on the line of separation between the sexes, we recall that the Antichrist, the "Man of Sin" of the last days, is distinctly stated by Daniel to have no "regard for the love of women."* Almost every earthly conqueror heretofore has been made weak through woman's love or lust; but here we are told that the devil's great masterpiece will be of another mind altogether. He will have nothing to do with the weaker sex. What does this mean? I think we have a *clew*. Let us follow it.

Daniel xi. 37. See also I. Timothy iv. 3.

Plate 22. WAITING HIS OPPORTUNITY.

THE WOMAN MOVEMENT.

We live in the midst of the greatest woman movement the world has ever seen in any age of which we have extensive history. On every side and in every way woman is coming to the front. It matters not what our opinions may be as to the merits of the case; the fact stares us in the face that the most prominent question before the great Christian denominations to-day is the woman question. General assembly and conference have their hands and their time pretty well filled in discussing what shall be done with woman in the church. Political parties are giving more and more of their attention to the influence of woman in their particular sphere. The W. C. T. U. has become already a tremendous political power. Law and medicine and art and science are open to her advances. Religious thought is not secure from her resistless invasion. Pulpits are calling her; publishers bow to her. These are sober facts that cannot be gainsaid; but in the midst of this general progress there is one fact of tremendous import that has escaped general attention. It is this:—

All the peculiar heresies that abound in the world to-day, especially those that deal with metaphysical distinctions and refinements, give strange prominence to woman. In fact, most of them exalt her to the office of priestess, so to speak. Theosophy has its Madame Blavatsky and Annie Besant; Christian Science has "Rev." Mrs. Dr. Eddy; Spiritualism has its legions of female *media;* Electrical Spirit Romance has Marie Correlli; Humanitarianism has Mrs. Ward; "Christian Socialism" has Katherine Wood; and in every department of thought a strange and singular prominence is given to woman. There seems to be a dangerous tendency to almost deify woman. Years ago I pointed out the certainty that the great W. C. T. U. would run dangerously near the rocks in the inevitable pursuit of woman's exaltation. Recently, in the city of Boston, at the Tremont Temple, one enthusiastic admirer shouted out: "Francis Willard, right or wrong; that is my creed." The applause was general, and while much of it was undoubtedly due to the popular estimation of that excellent lady, yet it was enough to cause one who has been watching the trend of the age to ponder on the possibilities before us.

Many of my readers have never heard or read the vagaries of the Theosophs. Were they an insignificant sect, few in numbers, we might dismiss their wild utterances as the ravings of madmen. But when we find publishing houses existing on the issuing of books by their favorite writers, some of which books have been priced at five dollars a volume, and yet sold in the thousands in a short time after publication, we begin to suspect that they are more influential than we had supposed. And it will be news to some who read these lines to be told that these people talk of the failure of the second Adam, and look for a second Eve, a female Messiah who will soon come and redeem the race from sin and suffering. Let me quote freely from one of their best books, a vision of one of the writers. I will give it very closely, though not in the exact language of the book, as I have not got it by me.

"In my vision I saw what seemed to be a great

temple of *Moslem architecture* [italics mine]. As I gazed upon it I heard a mighty voice from the heavens cry out, 'Worship God alone!' The interior of the temple appeared to be hidden by a heavy veil, and the voice cried, 'Take away the veil of idolatry!' With a strong effort I rent away the veil, and saw Buddha, surrounded by millions of worshippers. And presently he passed from sight. The second veil was very heavy, *heavier than the first, and it was deep red.* Again the voice was heard, crying, 'Take away the veil of blood!' With a stronger effort this, too, was rent away, and I saw Jesus, surrounded by a still greater crowd of worshippers. And he, too, passed away. The sight was still obstructed by a third veil, *heavier and darker than either of the others.* And the voice cried, 'Take away the *Curse of Eve!*' When this veil was rent by a last mighty effort, I saw a beautiful woman, seated on a white elephant, whose trappings glittered in a stream of light that fell from the sky above her. And, as I watched, she slowly ascended into the heavens; and the great voice cried, 'Worship God alone!'"

Remember, that this vision closes a book that professes to tell how to "Find Christ." Remember, also, that in all the long centuries of the Scripture history *God never once ordained a priestess*, while every heathen religion provided them in unlimited quantities. And only once in thousands of years did the Almighty sanction the *rule* of a woman, and that was *permitted* in the chaotic days when Deborah briefly gave direction to the affairs of state and church. The most rabid advocates of *extreme* "Woman's Rights" cannot blot out these facts. They will not down. But at this time, not only is woman brought to the front in the boldest manner, but there is also an undeniable tendency to exalt the celibate state as superior to the union of the sexes in marriage;* and with this comes a strange whisper of a mysterious sex union in the individual, or in some darkly mystical "spiritual" sense. Let us not forget that there were two sexes needed in the ark to go through the flood of water, and there will be

---

* Numbers of **hitherto useful** Christians have become tainted with this **heresy in the last few years.** ("Forbidding to marry." I. Timothy iv.)

needed both to go through the flood of fire so soon to visit the earth.

The result of this tendency to separate woman from man, and make her independent, is twofold. Man rebels against it, of course, and troubles without number follow. If my readers had before them a tithe of the information that has come in my way on this point, there would be no need to write further. Families are broken up, separations made final, happiness destroyed, business schemes frustrated, peace transformed into war, and calm into storm in hundreds and even thousands of cases. The heart instinctively hides most of such pains and agonies, and the public only becomes acquainted with the final outward effects. These are bad enough, and frequent enough to attract considerable attention; and many are the articles written and solutions offered on the problem of domestic relations.

I stand boldly out before the men and women of my age and generation, and charge directly upon this modern undue exaltation of woman, the real cause that makes " marriage a failure," in thousands of instances at least.

THE SEX QUESTION. 209

But I must not anticipate. The other effect of this movement is on woman's side. She is originally constituted to cling to a stronger nature, and as she turns away from man, Satan is ready to take advantage of this instinct, and provides a "spirit lover" ready to her hand. In one of the most popular of recent novels the heroine is depicted as not caring for men, nor the hero for women. Each has a wonderful spirit affinity whose transcendent attractions lift them far above all earthly and human loves. So plainly is this thought expressed that, in one place, some one comes in and sings a song, with the line,

"The woman wailing for her demon lover." *

This book was selling in the sixty thousands a short time after its issue, and many people wrote to the authoress to tell her how *clear* she had made the "horrid doctrine of the blood atonement" to their minds. Mark! The undue ex-

* See frontispiece. The heroine is constantly trying to carve a statue of her spirit lover, but without success. She is seen in her studio, standing before the unfinished figure, with outstretched arms, apparently in conversation with an unseen being, and the friend who discovers her sings the refrain quoted above.

altation of woman in a strange intercourse with the spirit world, and the tearing down of the central work of Jesus — a real antichrist writing, not very much disguised. The *clew* is growing.

But I hear some one say in amazement: "You do not mean to assert that human beings can have sexual intercourse with spirits?" I reply: Remember the serious words of Mr. Stead, quoted on page 159. They were written after much investigation, and meant that some people have had experiences which seem to be of this very nature. In plain English Mr. Stead meant this and nothing else. And I am prepared to assert, after the accumulation of evidence as conclusive as it could well be, that this is certainly true. More than that, it is much more widely known and practiced than most persons are prepared to believe without a great deal of examination into the facts in the case.

(I have the testimony of the most reliable witnesses that some persons, while rolling on the ground in the so-called "trances" at the fanatical meetings held by the notorious Mrs. Woodworth in California in 1890, were seen to be under the most powerful sexual excitement and evident gratification. But the incredulous reader exclaims, "They were unconscious, and it may, as Mr. Stead says, have been 'purely objective!'"* Wait a moment. I have in my possession a long letter, written by a woman who was at one time prominent in religious work and teaching. She writes many pages to explain to another woman all about this strange sexual gratification with an unseen being. To her it had come as an "angel of light," and perverted the beautiful Scriptures that speak of the closeness of the communion with the Lord under the type of the marriage relation. Such verses as "Thy Maker is thy husband," and the figures of Solomon's song were *taken literally*, and the deluded writer describes *how* this wonderful state of "communion" can be attained. She declares that it is "precisely like the experience of intercourse between a married couple." Of the methods I will not speak, for fear the devil might

---

* Read again the statements or confessions of the spirits quoted on page 174 about "using the human body with all its organs and faculties."

get the advantage of some weak reader if I did. Suffice it to say that the fundamental principle of the entire and deliberate *resignation of the will* to the "spirit" is strongly enforced, just as it is in all attempts to become a spirit medium. Do not turn away in utter incredulity. *I am relating awful but tremendous facts.* Wherever I go, and generally speak against such impurities even in the careful language necessary before a mixed audience, some one comes to me and tells me of the prevalence of these things among the people, or of their own enslavement by them. But let us look farther into the Scriptures on this point.

I have already quoted the words of Paul in Colossians ii. 18, "Beware lest any man beguile you into a voluntary humility, and worshipping of demons, intruding into those things which he hath not seen, vainly puffed up in his fleshly mind." Notice the word "fleshly." It is significant. And this warning is for the church in all ages, certainly for these days in which we live.

In I. Corinthians xi. 10, we find a most singular passage: "For this cause ought the woman to

Plate 23. THE SEDUCTION.

have power on her head because of the angels." Read the context and you will see that it contains a special discussion of the proper headship of man over woman, and that the whole thing is referred to the fall in Eden.

Why is this? All things have a reason. Let us look farther. In I. Samuel xxviii. 7, we read of a woman who "was the mistress of a demon." I give the literal sense of the Hebrew. The words in the English, "hath a familiar spirit" do not reveal the truth of the original. This phrase occurs many times in the Old Testament, and really means exactly instead of "a woman who hath a familiar spirit," "a woman, the mistress of a demon." And the word "mistress" has all the unclean significance that it has in English when we say that a woman is the mistress of a man.

To the objector I say. What are you going to do about it? Is the Bible inspired? Did God know the facts when he allowed men to write so? Here has been, for thousands of years, this plain declaration of the Word of God that this very intercourse between women and spirits was not only possible, but was an actual fact. I had been inclined to doubt the existence of such things in the case of the male sex; but at the close of this lecture in San Francisco, a man of sixty years of age came to me and said, "I am in that very state now, and have been for years. What can I do to get rid of them?" He insisted that this was so. Certainly God said that the "man who is a wizard" should be treated as a "witch"; and again we read of a "*man* or a woman that hath a familiar spirit." See Leviticus xviii. 19–27, and xx. 5, 6. *Is the Bible true or false?*

In the light of this revelation who cannot see *why* the Almighty decreed that, "Ye shall not suffer a witch to live." The fate of such a wretch was to be "stoned with stones." Leviticus xx. 27. Have you ever thought that the belief which dismisses the women of this class in the Bible times to the company of idiots and superstitious fanatics makes out a most terrible case of judgment against the Almighty? Is God a God who pronounces sentence of death upon an idiot simply for his lunacy? Does the God of Moses and of Abraham make such a frightful mistake as to kill people for a piece of ignorant superstition? **Are** we going to class our God with the witch burners of Massachusetts, and even the fanatical **Africans** in their fear of the "hoodoo"? Well, this is the **inexorable** conclusion of the matter if we insist on believing that the witches of Moses' time were simply self-deceived. There is no escape from this; no corner into which to crawl. Here are the hard facts. God specially singled out these sins as the sins of the Canaanites. He specially warned his people against them, **and declared** that on account of these sins he destroyed seven nations, men, women, and children. He specially sentenced in advance any man or woman who should enter into this mysterious intercourse with spirits; and that sentence was death, without appeal. Enough of the details of the worship of Astarte, the special goddess of the Canaanites, has come down to us to fill us with horror at its unspeakable filthiness. **But as we put all** these things together, what sane man can fail **to see** that such sweeping destruction demands a sufficient **reason.** No wonder the infidels, like Ingersoll and Paine, have pitched upon this as an evidence of cruelty on the part of the Almighty. I unhesitatingly declare that the church has never had a wholly sufficient answer to this charge, because it has not opened its eyes to the real depths of the sins mentioned. I know that the answers given have always been along the line of the vileness of the people of Canaan, but this deeper iniquity has been overlooked.

But suppose we see that there were seven nations, occupying the land, who were saturated through and through with this crowning sin. Suppose we conceive of a people whose very blood was poisoned by demon intercourse, until the children were tainted with the blood of hell. Cannot anyone see that the utter destruction of such a demon-infected spawn was the only possible way to purify the land? I insist on it, every effect must have an adequate cause, and every act of the center of all reason must have a consistent reason behind it. "Cruelty!" did you say? What greater evidence of kindness, on the part of an all-powerful ruler, to thoroughly disinfect a fever-smitten climate before taking his own people into it? What stronger proof of the love of God than this arbitrary destruction of the works of the devil? So a little common-sense study of the truth turns this favorite weapon of the infidel squarely against himself, and presents another unanswerable demonstration of the marvelous mercy of the God of Love.

CHAPTER II.

The Sin of the Angels.

TO settle all doubts as to the existence and activity of angels, good and bad, read in Daniel of the "Prince of Persia" who "withstood" the messenger of God, and of "Michael your Prince" who came to the rescue. Remember how Satan contended with Michael for the body of Moses in Jude; the story of Ahab's lying prophets in Kings and Chronicles; the personal appearance of Satan in Job's case; the "Watcher and the holy one" who decreed the punishment of Nebuchadnezzar; the angel in Egypt, at Jericho, at the threshing floor of Ornan, at the destruction of Sennacherib's host, and of the host about Elisha at Dothan, and of the "twelve legions" for which Jesus could have prayed. Nothing is plainer in Scripture than the personality of good and of evil angels, and of their interference in the affairs of men. (See Hebrews i. 13, 14, and Mark i. 24.)

Jesus said, "As it was in the days of Noah . . . . and as it was in the days of Lot, so shall it be in the days of the Son of Man." We have hastily concluded that the only reference here is to the suddenness of the destruction that overtook the people of those periods. But this is a serious mistake. Christ evidently meant to compare the general and particular characteristics of those early times with the last days. It behooves us to inquire what were the special features of the times referred to. In the days of Noah we see four conspicuous characteristics: 1. The multiplicity of sciences and inventions, produced by the sinful line of Cain, in their effort to make the world tolerable in spite of the curse. 2. The sin of the wicked angels with the women of the time. 3. The preparation of the ark, and the preaching of Noah (preceded by that of Enoch). 4. The carelessness and indifferent unbelief of the race in general towards all warning.

Certainly it is easy to see the reproduction of the first of these great signs Such an age of invention the world never saw before. This will pass without a question from anyone. The third and fourth signs are very distinctly marked. Many are diligently preaching the near coming of the Lord, but the great mass refuse to hear. The public prints ridicule us, and caricature the solemn descriptions of awful judgments. A San Francisco leading daily recently gave two columns to an absurd article on my lectures, picturing the baseball players of that city in the act of striking at the fiery meteors, which God's word declares shall, and which science frankly admits may, at any time largely destroy this earth and most of its wicked inhabitants. Even the most careful utterances of men like Dr. A. J. Gordon, of Boston, are ridiculed in the same way by the great majority. It all serves to prove the truth of the Scripture to the careful student, and shows how generally the race is ripening for the last great cataclysm. Eating, drinking, marrying and giving in marriage, buying, selling, planting, building; how the world is filled with these schemes and efforts after earthly happiness!) And what a general weakening of the old standards of faith! "Higher Criticism!" Heaven save the mark! Anything to lower faith in the plain word of God from which "not one jot or tittle shall pass away till all be fulfilled."

The second sign is here, whatever the incredulous may say; and the proof of this is one of the chief purposes of this book Before passing to this proof it is well to remember Sodom, and think of the great distinguishing characteristic of filthy sins which have been stamped even upon the name of the city. From those days to these, sodomy has been regarded as one of the worst and most degrading of all sins; yet the worst has not been realized. We turn now to ask, if the last days are to be marked by the reproduction of those sins of Sodom and of the wicked angels, what were those sins? Have we any reliable record of them? Certainly we have; but its study will probably prove a surprise to many faithful readers of the Scriptures.

Peter speaks at length of the sins of uncleanness which are to mark the last days. In II. Peter ii. we read: "But there were false prophets also among the people, *even as there shall be false teachers among you*, who privily [that is, in disguise] shall bring in damnable heresies, even denying the Lord that bought them [all of the 'isms' do sooner or later]. . . . . And many shall follow their pernicious ways [warrant here for my assertions that these things are not merely the ravings of a few]; by reason of whom the truth shall be evil spoken of. [How this is coming true! Because of these imitations the greatest amount of discredit is cast on the truth. The power and willingness of God to heal in answer to the 'prayer of faith' is sneered at because of the false imitations under various names.] . . . . But if God spared not the angels that sinned, but cast them down to hell [the word is *Tartarus*, the only place it occurs. It seems to mean the outer confines of the universe. Note this in connection with my comment on the 'great chain' of revelation, and the binding of Satan* away from the earth in the

---

* See "Alpha and Omega.

Plate 24.   THE FALL ACCOMPLISHED.

THE SIN OF THE ANGELS.

'bottomless pit'], and delivered them unto chains of darkness to be reserved unto judgment; and spared not the old world, but delivered Noah, the eighth person,* a preacher of righteousness, bringing in the flood upon the world of the ungodly; and turning the cities of Sodom and Gomorrah into ashes, condemned them with an overthrow, making them an ensample unto those that should live ungodly. . . . . The Lord knoweth how to deliver the godly out of temptations, and to reserve the unjust unto the day of judgment to be punished; but chiefly those that walk after the

---

* I cannot forbear a brief note here on the marvels of the numbers of the Bible. Why is Noah called the "eighth person"? Eight is the number of the new life. Following the perfect seven, it speaks of a new beginning. So the number of the name of Jesus (that is, the sum of the numbers for which the Greek letters stand) is eight hundred and eighty-eight. In this threefold repetition we have the greatest intensity; just as the six hundred and sixty-six of the "Beast" gives the intensive of the number six, the number of sin. Now Noah is peculiarly a type of the new birth, a new life, in that he came through the flood — the washing of regeneration for the world — to begin the new life on the hither side. So we find the number of the new life, eight, stamped in everything about him. Thus: the year of the flood, 1656, the forty days' rain, the one hundred and twenty years of preaching, the eight in the ark, the cubical contents of the ark, the total time in the ark, — all these are perfect multiples of eight. And when we turn to his name, according to one spelling, we have fifty-six, or seven times eight; and the other spelling gives eight times eight. So wonderfully are the typical records written everywhere.

flesh in the lust of uncleanness. . . . . Spots they are and blemishes . . . . having eyes full of adultery, and that cannot cease from sin; beguiling unstable souls; an heart they have exercised with covetous practices; cursed children, which have forsaken the right way, and are gone astray, following the way of Balaam, the son of Bosor, who loved the wages of unrighteousness; but was rebuked for his iniquity; the dumb ass speaking with man's voice forbade the madness of the prophet. (Note this specially). . . . . These are wells without water, clouds that are carried with a tempest, to whom is reserved the mist of darkness forever. . . . . They allure through the lusts of the flesh, through much wantonness . . . . while they promise them liberty, they themselves are the servants of corruption." How these errors of to-day promise the liberty of the deep knowledge in their possession! The inspired writer here most distinctly classes the "sin of the angels" and the sins of Sodom and Gomorrah with the filthy sensualities of the teachers which were to come in the future. No one can deny this, for there it is in plain language. You may question inspiration, but not the existence of the record. Our eyes can read it for ourselves.

But another witness has arisen in these last days. The Book of Enoch is now in our possession, and can be read by all. The early Christian Fathers quoted freely from this book, and seemed to think it genuine in the main. Long ago it was lost to the world of letters, but in the latter part of the last century Bruce, the great African traveler, found two copies of it in Ethiopia, and brought them to England. About 1825 Archbishop Lawrence translated it into English, and it excited a great deal of notice and comment. Somewhere in the early seventies (1872 I think) a revision was made by a learned Englishman, the author of "The Evolution of Christianity"; and only three years ago still another has been issued from the Andover press in Massachusetts. Now it is singular that this book contains in full the account of the "sin of the angels," and details how Enoch was sent by God to preach to them, and pronounce judgment upon them for their mighty wickedness. Here we find all those remarkable names for the angels that Milton uses in his Paradise Lost, for the names of the principal leaders of the satanic hosts are given with some minuteness. The sin is distinctly described as being a sexual union with the women of the time. Only this, nothing more. If there is any part of the book that is genuine, it is undoubtedly the first part, in which this description occurs. The latter portion of the book seems to bear the evidences of having been added a long time after. In this book is found the famous prophecy of Enoch quoted by the apostle Jude. But it is well to quote the story in full.

BOOK OF ENOCH — CHAPTER VII. *

1. It happened after the sons of men had multiplied in those day, that daughters were born to them, elegant and beautiful.

---

* The editor argues powerfully for the truth of much of the book; he shows that it is undoubtedly of Hebrew origin, and certainly comes from a period long before the time of Christ. He admits the admixture of the false, but concludes that we "must inevitably enroll Enoch among the prophets, or reconsider the supernatural in Christianity."

THE SIN OF THE ANGELS.

2. And when the angels, the sons of heaven, beheld them, they became enamoured of them, saying to each other, Come, let us select for ourselves wives from the progeny of men, and let us beget children.

3. Then their leader, Samyaza, said to them, I fear that you may perhaps be indisposed to the performance of this enterprise;

4. And that I alone shall suffer for so grievous a crime.

5. But they answered him and said, We all swear;

6. And bind ourselves by mutual execrations, that we will not change our intentions, but execute our projected undertaking.

7. Then they all swore together, and all bound themselves by mutual execrations. Their whole number was two hundred, who descended upon Ardis, which is the top of Mount Armon.

8. That mountain was therefore called Armon, because they had sworn upon it, and bound themselves by mutual execrations.

9. These are the names of their chiefs: Sam-

yaza, who was their leader, Urakabaramcel, Azibeel, Tamiel, Ramuel, Danel, Azkeel, Saraknyal, Asael, Armers, Batrael, Yomyael, Arazyal. These were the prefects of the two hundred angels, and the remainder were all with them.

10. Then they took wives; each choosing for himself; whom they began to approach, and with whom they cohabited; teaching them sorcery, incantations, and the dividing of roots and trees.

11. And the women conceiving brought forth giants,

12. Whose stature was each three hundred cubits.* These devoured all which the labor of men produced; until it became impossible to feed them;

14. And began to injure birds and beasts, reptiles, and fishes, to eat their flesh one after another, and to drink their blood.

15. Then the earth reproved the unrighteous.

CHAPTER VIII.

1. Moreover, Azazyel taught men to make swords, knives, shields, breastplates, the fabrica-

---

* Scripture says distinctly that the offspring of this unnatural union were "giants." This, however, does not require us to accept the "three hundred cubits." The basis of fact is one thing; the enveloping exaggeration is another. — *R. K. C.*

tion of mirrors, and the workmanship of bracelets and ornaments, the use of paints, the beautifying of the eyebrows, the use of stones of every valuable and select kind, and all sorts of dyes, so that the world became altered.

2. Impiety increased; fornication multiplied; and they transgressed and corrupted all their ways.

3. Amazarak taught all the sorcerers and dividers of roots.

4. Armers taught the solution of sorcery.

5. Barkayal taught the observers of the stars.

6. Akibeel taught signs.

7. Tamiel taught astronomy.

8. And Asradel taught the motion of the moon.

9. And men, being destroyed, cried out; and their voice reached unto heaven.

CHAPTER IX.

1. Then Michael, and Gabriel, Raphael, Suryal, and Uriel looked down from heaven and saw the quantity of blood which was shed upon the earth. and said. . . . to their Lord, the King.

5. Thou hast seen what Azazyel has done, how

he has taught every species of iniquity upon the earth. . . .

6. Samyaza also has taught sorcery, to whom thou hast given authority over those who are associated with him. They have gone together to the daughters of men; have lain with them; have become polluted.

7. And have discovered crimes to them.

8. The women likewise have brought forth giants.

9. Thus the whole earth has been filled with blood and iniquity. (Then the Lord sent a messenger to Noah and gave him warning of the flood.)

CHAPTER X.

6. Again the Lord said to Raphael, bind Azazyel hand and foot; cast him into darkness. . . .*

8. There shall he remain forever; cover his face that he may not see the light.

9. And in the great day of judgment let him be cast into the fire.

11. All the earth shall not perish in conse-

* II. Peter ii. 4.

Plate 25.   THE BIRTH OF FEAR.

quence of every secret by which the watchers have destroyed, and which they have taught their offspring.

13. To Gabriel the Lord said, Go to the biters, the reprobates, to the children of fornication; and destroy the children of fornication, the offspring of the watchers from among men.

To Michael likewise the Lord said, Go and announce his crime to Samyaza, and to the others who are with him, who have been associated with women, that they might be polluted with all their impurity. And when all their sons shall be slain, when they shall see the perdition of their beloved, bind them for seventy generations underneath the earth, even to the day of judgment, and of consummation, until the judgment, the effect of which shall last forever, be completed.

16. Then shall they be taken away into the lowest depths of the fire in torments; and in confinement shall they be shut up forever.

18. Destroy all the souls addicted to dalliance, and the offspring of the watchers, for they have tyrannized over mankind.

CHAPTER XII.

5. Then the Lord said to me: Enoch, scribe of righteousness, Go tell the watchers of heaven, who have deserted the lofty sky, and their holy everlasting station, who have been polluted with women.

6. And have done as the sons of men do, by taking to themselves wives, and who have been greatly corrupted upon the earth;

7. That on the earth they shall never obtain peace and remission of sin. For they shall not rejoice in their offspring; they shall behold the slaughter of their beloved; shall lament for the destruction of their sons; and petition forever; but shall not obtain mercy and peace.*

CHAPTER XIII.

1. Then Enoch, passing on, said to Azazyel, Thou shalt not obtain peace. A great sentence has gone forth against thee;

2. Neither shall relief, mercy and supplication be thine, on account of the oppression which thou hast taught;

* II. Peter ii. 9.

THE SIN OF THE ANGELS.

3. And on account of every act of blasphemy, tyranny, and sin which thou hast taught to the children of men;

4. Then departing from him I spoke to them all together;

5. And they all became terrified and trembled;*

6. Beseeching me to write for them a memorial of supplication, etc.

Enoch then had a wonderful vision in which he saw the Lord in heaven, and one whom he describes in language similar to that employed in Scripture in relation to Christ. The punishment of the watchers was reaffirmed, and then the voice of the Lord called Enoch near, and

CHAPTER XV.

1. Then, addressing me, He spoke and said, Hear, neither be afraid, O righteous Enoch, thou scribe of righteousness: Approach hither and hear my voice. Go, say to the watchers of heaven, who have sent thee to pray for them, You ought to pray for men, and not men for you.

* James ii. 19.

2. Wherefore have you forsaken the lofty and holy heaven, which endures forever, and have lain with women; have defiled yourselves with the daughters of men; have taken to yourselves wives; have acted like the sons of earth, and have begotten impious offspring?

3. You being spiritual, holy, and possessing a life which is eternal, have polluted yourselves with women, have begotten in carnal blood, have lusted in the blood of men, have done as those do who are flesh and blood.

4. These however die and perish.

5. Therefore have I given to them wives, that they might cohabit with them, that sons might be born of them, and that this might be transacted upon the earth.

6. But you, from the beginning were made spiritual, possessing a life which is eternal, and not subject to death forever.

7. Therefore I made not wives for you, because being spiritual your dwelling is in heaven.

8. Now the giants, who were born of spirit and flesh, shall be called on earth evil spirits,

and earth shall be their habitation. Evil spirits shall proceed from their flesh, because they were created from above; from the holy watchers was their beginning and primary foundation. Evil spirits shall they be upon earth, and the spirits of the wicked shall they be called.

9. The spirits of the giants shall be like clouds,* which shall oppress, corrupt, fall, contend, and bruise upon the earth.

CHAPTER XVI.

1. And as to the death of the giants, wheresoever their spirits depart from their bodies, let their flesh, that which is perishable, be without judgment. Thus shall they perish until the day of the great consummation of the great world.

2. And now to the watchers, who have sent thee to pray for them, who in the beginning were in heaven,

3. Say, In heaven have you been; secret things, however, have not been manifested to you; yet have you known a reprobated mystery.

4. And this have you related to women in the

---
* II. Peter ii. 17.

hardness of your heart, and by that mystery* have women and mankind multiplied evils upon the earth.

5. Say to them, Never therefore shall you obtain peace.

CHAPTER XIX.

1. Then Uriel said, Here the angels who cohabited with women, appointed their leaders;

2. And being numerous in appearance made men profane, and caused them to err; so that they sacrificed to devils as to God.† For in the great day there shall be a judgment, with which they shall be judged, until they are consumed; and their wives also shall be judged, who led astray the angels of heaven that they might salute them.

CHAPTER XXI.

1. Then I made a circuit to a place where nothing was completed, a desolate spot, prepared and terrific.

3. There too I beheld seven stars of heaven bound together, like great mountains, and like

---
* Revelation xvii. 5; and II. Thessalonians ii. 7.
† I. Corinthians x. 20.

blazing fire. I exclaimed, for what species of crime have they been bound, and why have they been removed to this place? Then Uriel, one of the holy angels who was with me, and conducted me, answered: Enoch, these are those of the stars which have transgressed the commandment of the most high God; and are here bound, until the infinite number of the days of their crimes be completed.

5. I beheld the preparation of a great fire blazing and glittering, in the midst of which there was a division. Columns of fire struggled together to the end of the abyss, and deep was their descent. But neither its measurement nor magnitude was I able to discover; neither could I perceive its origin. Then I exclaimed, How terrible is this place, and how difficult to explore.

6. Uriel, one of the holy angels who was with me, answered and said: Enoch, why art thou alarmed and amazed at this terrific place, at the sight of this place of suffering? This, he said, is the prison of the angels; and here they are kept forever.*

* Revelation xx. 10. Jude 6.

CHAPTER LIII.

1. Then I looked and turned myself to another part of the earth, where I beheld a deep valley burning with fire.

3. And there my eyes beheld the instruments which they were making, fetters of iron without weight.

4. Then I inquired of the angel of peace, who proceeded with me, saying, For whom are these fetters and instruments prepared?

5. He replied, These are prepared for the host of Azazyel, that they may be delivered over and adjudged to the lowest condemnation; and that their angels may be overwhelmed with hurled stones, as the Lord of spirits has commanded.

6. Michael and Gabriel, Raphael and Phanuel shall be strengthened in that day, and shall cast them into a furnace of blazing fire, that the Lord of spirits may be avenged of them for their crimes; because they became ministers of Satan, and seduced them who dwell upon the earth.

CHAPTER LXVI.

4. And they shall confine those angels who disclosed impiety.

6. And when all this was effected .... the fluid mass of fire .... and the valley of the angels who had been guilty of seduction.

7. Through that valley also rivers of fire were flowing, to which those angels shall be condemned, who seduced the inhabitants of the earth.

9. Their spirits shall be full of revelry, that they may be judged in their bodies; because they have denied the Lord of spirits

12. Judgment has come upon them, because they trusted in their carnal revelry, and denied the Lord of spirits.

CHAPTER LXVII.

2. At that time holy Michael answered and said to Raphael, The severity of the judgment, of the secret judgment of the angels, who is capable of beholding the endurance of that severe judgment which has taken place and been made permanent without being melted at the sight?

4. They shall not be before the eye of the Lord; since the Lord of spirits has been offended with them; for like Lords have they conducted themselves. Therefore will he bring upon them a secret judgment for ever and ever.

5. For neither shall angel nor man receive a portion of it; but they alone shall receive their own judgment for ever and ever.

CHAPTER LXVIII.

1. After this judgment they shall be astonished and irritated; for it shall be exhibited to the inhabitants of the earth.

2. Behold the names of those angels. These are their names. The first is Samyaza; the second, Aristikapha; the third Armen, etc., ... the twenty-first, Azazyel.

4. The name of the first is Yekun; he it was who seduced all the sons of the holy angels; and causing them to descend to the earth, led astray the offspring of men.

5. The name of the second is Kesabel, who pointed out evil counsel to the sons of the holy

Plate 26. THE FIRST SHAME.

angels, and induced them to corrupt their bodies by generating mankind

6. The name of the third is Gadrel: he discovered every stroke of death to the children of men.

7. *He seduced Eve;* and discovered to the children of men the instruments of death.

17. The name of the fifth is Kasyade: he discovered to the children of men every wicked stroke of spirits and demons.

18. The stroke of the embryo in the womb to diminish it; the stroke of the spirit by the bite of the serpent, etc.

CHAPTER LXXXIII — ENOCH'S PRAYER.

5. The angels of heaven have transgressed; and on mortal flesh shall thy wrath remain till the day of the great judgment.

6. Now then, O God, Lord, and mighty King, I entreat thee, and beseech thee to grant my prayer, that a posterity may be left to me on earth, and that *the whole human race may not perish.*

A part only of these quotations from Enoch have

been known for centuries, while the complete manuscript of the book was lost to Europe, the part being found in a Greek fragment quoted by Syncellus. It is generally conceded that Milton's ideas were obtained from the book of Enoch, or from those floating phrases and names which had come down to his day. We are compelled to admit that this Sin of the Angels is the most important thing in the book, excepting perhaps the fragment quoted by Jude. Even this fragment, however, was written of the sinning angels and of such men as should follow in their evil ways. The remarkable resemblance between the quotations and passages in Jude and Peter have been hastily pointed out in our foot notes. We are now ready for the sacred Canon again, and in natural sequence take up the book of Jude.

The little book of Jude is a most singular one. I do not hesitate to say that most people let it alone with the feeling that they do not understand it. And yet its language is plain enough, if taken in its simple literal sense. *The trouble has been that few, if any, were prepared to believe the things* which the apostle states, but brushed them aside *as figures of speech*. Now, in the light of what we have been considering, let us read it, with simple directness, and see what he really says.

After his address, "to them that are sanctified by God the Father, and preserved in Jesus Christ, and called," he goes on to state the *purpose* of the book, "that ye should earnestly contend for the faith which was once delivered unto the saints."

Here is a note of alarm, the sound of the bugle through the camp. If the bugle blow, it means that the enemy is at hand. Then he should say something of the approach of the foe. That is precisely what he does say in the next place; and, in saying it, he gives the *reason* why this contention is needed.

"For there are certain men crept in unawares, who were before of old ordained to this condemnation." Immediately we ask, What have these men done? What is their line of attack? The answer is ready: "Ungodly men, *turning the grace of our God into lasciviousness*, and denying the only Lord God, and our Lord Jesus Christ." Remember what I have written of those who change the beautiful marriage figures of Scripture into a literal thing, and then think whether such do not "turn the grace of our God into lasciviousness?" Could any description be plainer?

But was this a new thing in the days of Jude? Read on. "I will, *therefore*, put you in remembrance, though *ye once knew this*, how that the Lord, having saved the people out of the land of Egypt, afterward destroyed them that believed not. And the angels which kept not their first estate [principality], but left their own habitation, he hath reserved in everlasting chains under darkness unto the judgment of the great day." How like to Peter's description this is. Evidently both wrote of the same thing. So we have two inspired witnesses. But we now see that Jude has compared these "men who had crept in unawares" to the "angels that sinned." Manifestly the only point of comparison is in the nature of the sin. Then does he say what the sin of either was? If he does, we can at once determine the sin of the other. Yes, the Apostle expressly describes what the "sin of the angels" was. He says, "Even as Sodom and Gomorrah and the cities about them, in like manner [to the angels and the men who had crept into the church], giving themselves over to fornication, and *going after strange flesh* [other flesh], are set forth as an example, suffering the vengeance of eternal fire."

Now there can be no possible mistake about this language. Jude certainly declares that the angels sinned by committing fornication, and committing it with strange flesh; that is, not with their own kind. And he as plainly states that this was what the frightful sinners of the cities of the plain did also. Lest there should be any doubt about his application to the present state of the church he proceeds to assert that the men who had crept in were doing this same unutterable thing. Here it is in the next verse.

"Likewise, also, these filthy dreamers defile the flesh, despise dominion, and speak evil of dignities." Notice the exact language here very closely. He calls the men who had crept in, "filthy dreamers." When we remember that most of these awful iniquities are practiced in a sort of trance, or "dream," the wording of the Apostle becomes doubly significant.* And he expressly declares that "they defile the flesh" in the *very same manner* as did the citizens of Sodom and the fallen angels.

Again, in verse 10, he further touches on the nature of their sin. "But what they know naturally as brute beasts, in those things they corrupt themselves." Here is a clear statement that the thing in which they sinned was the sexual passion. And note that they did not find this passion wrong in itself, but sinned by "corrupting" it; that is, by using it out of its place, as the "brute beast" never does. Mark this well.

The next particular is very significant. The Apostle says that these "filthy dreamers" have "gone in the way of Cain." Did this mean merely that some of them were murderers? I think the meaning is much deeper than that. Let us remember it. Next they are compared to Balaam,

---

* Examples of this can be given by the score, and these "dreamers" are all too ready to teach others how to experience the same.

THE SIN OF THE ANGELS. 255

as in the words of Peter.* Notice that Peter also compares them to "natural brute beasts," and speaks of the good angels not bringing railing accusations against them, just as Jude does. The two evidently wrote of the very same thing.

Hear Jude speak of them, you who may in some way be tempted by the adroit solicitation to explore deep things, and learn the mysteries. He says, "These are spots in your feasts of charity, when they feast with you, feeding themselves without fear; clouds they are without water, carried about of winds; trees whose fruit withereth, without fruit, twice dead, plucked up by the roots; raging waves of the sea, foaming out of their own shame; wandering stars, to whom is reserved the blackness of darkness forever." Reader! if any-one ever begins to tell you of any possible literal interpretation of the marriage figures of the Scriptures, or to apply them to the physical body in any connection whatever with the sex principle, *run for your life; stay not in all the plain, but escape to the mountain!* These terrible words of the two

* See page 226.

Apostles are the most fearful in the whole Bible, and they are most unmistakably spoken of those who sin in the way of which I am writing. They are indeed terrible words, but they are spoken of terrible sins; in fact of the most fearful sin possible to the race, the sin which crowned the iniquity of the antediluvians, the sin which brought, "the iniquity of the Amorites to the full," and the sin which shall sum up the iniquity of the last days of this age in which we live. Is this hasty? No, read on.

We have seen that the book of Enoch records that prophet's message to the fallen angels, and expressly describes their sin to have been as just written. Now, in the next verse, Jude appeals to this very book, and quotes the marvelous man, who before the flood walked three long centuries with God, as speaking of these very men and angels. "And Enoch also, the seventh from Adam, prophesied of these [of these men, and Sodomites and angels], saying, Behold the Lord cometh with ten thousands of his saints to execute judgment upon all, and to convince all that are ungodly among

THE SIN OF THE ANGELS.

them of all their ungodly deeds which they have ungodly committed, and of all their hard speeches which ungodly sinners have spoken against him." Then Jude again states the nature of the sin by saying: "These are murmerers, complainers, walking after their own lusts; and their mouth speaking great swelling words, having men's persons in admiration because of advantage."*

This is certainly a very forcible description of the "great swelling words" in which the Esoterics and Theosophists seek to clothe their vague ideas. The language is often very imposing, but reminds me of a stunning fire of blank cartridges, — a tremendous noise, nothing hit, and ending in gas. But in this case, unfortunately, many are poisoned by the gas before it is dissipated. Jude does not leave the matter here, but goes on to say that this same sort of men shall be in the world in the last days.

"But beloved, remember ye the words which were spoken before of the Apostles of our Lord

---

* I suggest a close study of the original of the last sentence. Perhaps it means something deeper and viler than is at first credible.

Jesus Christ; how that they told you there shall be mockers in the last time [and what shall they do?] who should walk after their own ungodly lusts." But some one objects that this does not necessarily mean sexuality. Ah! the Apostle has provided for that. "These be they who *separate themselves, sensual,* having not the spirit." Here you have a plain description of the evils to which I have already alluded, the *separation* between man and woman, but a separation which is not really clean, but "sensual," because of the strange demon union that is connected with it. And hence the word "sensual" is fitly coupled with the "separation," indicating the real nature of the thing. The promise, given in "great swelling words," is to lead you into "deep mysteries," that shall reveal the most valuable truths to the seeker; but in order that this search may be effectual, you must "separate" yourselves from many natural affections and connections (forbidding to marry, etc.); on the ground that these things are too worldly and impure. The earnest seeker after the highest holiness is thus deluded, and is then ready

Plate 27. THE SENSE OF GUILT.

to be taught that the highest union of the spirit with the Lord can be made known when those other baser affections are set aside. In this disguise of "an angel of light" the "spirit love" is introduced, and the horrible results speedily follow; for such "have not the Spirit," that is, the spirit they do have is not the spirit of God, but a demon.

It is well to follow out the marginal references connected with Jude 19. Proverbs xviii. 1, says, "He that separateth himself seeketh according to his desire, and intermeddleth in every business. Ezekiel xiv. 6–8 speaks of a man "separating himself from me, and setting up his idols in his heart." Hosea iv. 14, says, "I will not punish your daughters when they commit whoredom, nor your spouses when they commit adultery: for themselves are separated with whores, and they sacrifice with harlots." Hosea ix. 10, reads, "I found Israel like grapes in the wilderness; I saw your fathers as the first ripe in the fig tree at her first time; but they went to Baal-peor, and separated themselves to that shame; and their abominations were according as they loved." Tertullian says (vol. 3, p. 22), "What will the flesh 'lust' after except what is more of the flesh? For which reason, in the beginning, it became estranged from the spirit. 'My spirit, saith God, shall not permanently abide in the men eternally, for that they are flesh.'"

These references abundantly connect the actions of the men spoken of with the great sin of the wilderness—the sin of Baal-peor, the nature of which we will further examine in the light of Scripture. I call special attention to these declarations of the Bible, and to the fact that a hasty dismissal of them, places the Christian in a very inconsistent position. As I said before, most readers of the Bible have not been ready to really believe what Jude and Peter declare. It has seemed so fanciful, so repulsive, so extraordinary, and so supernatural that the easiest way has been found in that ignoring of these verses altogether which has marked the general attitude of the church and certainly the knowledge of the average member.

To sum it up: Jude plainly states that in the

apostolic age there was great need for watchfulness on account of the **presence in** the church of certain men who were **turning the grace of God into lasciviousness.** These men were simply following in the footsteps of those who had **acted in a** similar manner shortly after the exodus from Egypt, and they all had imitated the example of the wicked angels, which angels, the Apostle states, were guilty of the very same sins as the people of Sodom—the sin of sexual intercourse with "other flesh," that is with creatures of another order of being.* He declares that those angels, for their terrible sin, **were and are reserved under chains of darkness until** the final day of judgment, being thus set forth as an example to the world. Note just here that an example is of no force if those **who are by it warned** cannot possibly follow it. There is no occasion **to warn me by** the sad fate of an eagle who attempted **to** fly across the **Atlantic Ocean and was** drowned, for I cannot fly at

---

* The **candid** reader **of** Genesis xix. must admit that the men of Sodom actually tried to capture **the two** angels who came to save Lot, and for the expressed purpose of unnatural intercourse with them. It was for this that the citizens were smitten with blindness.

all. In the same way the angels who had intercourse with human beings can be no possible example of warning to us unless we can attempt to imitate their example by seeking intercourse with angels. Surely this is the plainest common sense.

But Jude goes on to say in the most direct words that these "filthy dreamers" actually did "defile the flesh" in the very same way as did the wicked angels; that this way was by "corrupting" the otherwise normal animal passion common to men; and that the thing was identical with the "way of Cain" and with the error of "Baal-peor," as taught by the wicked prophet Balaam to the Israelites in the plains of Moab. He then thunders against the men then living who practiced these abominations, comparing them with the fallen angels, and consigning them to the same punishment, quotes from the book of Enoch—the special messenger of God to the angels, and therein declares that *such sinners will be found on earth at the second advent and be destroyed by the Lord at his appearing.* In speaking of these latter day apostates he uses the significant term "separate themselves sensual," which term is elsewhere employed in designating the sin of Baal-peor, thus clearly declaring that this monumental sin shall be practiced in the last days of the present dispensation.

The sin of Baal-peor stands unquestionably at **the very head of the** transgressions in the wilderness. **A careful examination of all** the references **to this iniquity** will convince the most skeptical of the vast importance attached to it by the Almighty. **Any** good commentary or Bible dictionary speaks **of the** worship of Baal as identical with that of the *phallus* or generative principle. **In this** connection it is well to remember **that the god Dagon, the deity of** the **Philistines, also** represented **the** generative **principle.** In a later chapter we discuss fully this worship, and its connection **with the** sign of the cross, **but** call attention here to the singular consistency of the punishments that were sent upon the Philistines when the ark of God was captured by them **and** placed in **the temple of Dagon,** whose wife was Atergatis, or Astarte — a goddess noted for the vile impurities of her worship.

In I. Samuel v. and vi., we find the story of the plagues sent on Philistia. The ark had been set up before Dagon, who was found upon his face the next morning. Being restored to his position, and the ark left before him again, in the morning he lay upon the threshold with his head and arms and hands severed from the trunk and fish's tail which terminated his figure. Then the plague of the emerods fell upon the people. The ark was moved to another place, but the same dreadful affliction followed it until the "cry of the city went up to heaven." These emerods (hemorrhoids?) were upon the "secret parts" of the Philistines. The signification is too obvious to be slighted. They who worshipped a god representing the generative organs and the generative principle, and who undertook to set this god above Jehovah, were thus smitten in those very organs by a terrible disease. Josephus says that their sufferings were awful, and that thousands died from the plague. I mention this to show that Baal-worship meant more than a mere superstitious idolatry, and to emphasize the references to the great wilderness sin found in both Jude and Peter, and incidentally noticed by several of the prophets always in such severe language.

Reviewing the parallel passage in II Peter ii. we see that he declares the very same things; that in the last days there shall be "false teachers" whose teaching he distinctly classes with that of Balaam, and with the sin of the angels who are cast down into Tartarus until the great judgment, and with the sin of Sodom and Gomorrah; and then uses almost the precise language of Jude with regard to their character and punishment. Even if we did not believe the Bible, all this falls into place very consistently with our present study; but if we do believe the Scriptures are inspired we are simply forced to accept the above plain facts as the positive teaching of the book. I again refer to the direct statements of the Old Testament that not only women but men had "familiar spirits," and remind the reader of the awful judgments pronounced by God against all such persons.

The whole matter reduces to this: The Bible repeatedly declares that women were "mistresses of demons," and even some men sustained some similar relationship with angelic creatures. God Almighty saw fit to exhaust language in denunciation of this terrific sin, and to assign the most severe conceivable punishments as penalties for its commission. After all the iniquities of Egypt, and the numerous backslidings by the way, the special sin which crowned the transgressions of the wilderness was that learned from Balaam and the women of Moab, which was identical with the "iniquity of the Amorites," for which the latter nation was exterminated from the earth; which sin is positively declared by parallel Scripture to be the same as that of Sodom and Gomorrah, this last being completely identified with the great sin of the wicked angels with the women of the antediluvian age. And finally, we are solemnly warned that this awful and mysterious transgression shall be repeated in the closing days of the present age, and shall be taught as a wonderful thing by "ministers of Satan," who come in the disguise of "angels of light."*

* I kindly urge upon the reader, and specially the objector, to soberly study this paragraph and the next one, over and over; then answer the query: Is the Bible true?

This whole matter is so closely interwoven with the very fabric of the Bible that it is difficult to see how it can be cut out without destroying the entire book. As we will see, it begins in Eden, is woven into the life of Cain and the antediluvians, stands closely connected with the deluge, reappears among the Sodomites and Canaanites, causes the destruction of the entire adult race of the exodus, exhibits symptoms of its virulence all along the history of the kingdom, manifests itself in the apostolic church, and is specified as one of the great signs of the last days of this age. Surely he who attempts to get rid of it must throw away his Bible altogether.

This is the lowest wickedness of which the race is capable. As I said before, *the worst sins are not wrought in the gutter and the brothel, but under the disguise of religion and philosophy and metaphysics.* " *Knowledge is power*" *in any direction, down as well as up.* Let the reader again remember that these are the careful utterances of two of the Apostles, and were both written for the last times of the age in which we certainly live. A frequent rehearsal of these two important facts will prove decidedly healthy. A hasty "pooh-pooh" is worse than foolish. If you do not believe the Bible to be the Word of God, you have some excuse; at least, the excuse of consistency. But if you pretend to consider it inspired, be careful that *you* be not included among the "scoffers,"* who make light of the "promises." Scoffing at the plain meaning of God's Word has always been a very dangerous thing.

As a sort of collateral testimony turn to the numerous myths of the marriages between the gods and women. Remember the story of Jupiter and Europa, of Diana and Endymion, of Venus and Adonis, and all the host of legends telling of the loves of the heathen deities, in which the element of a forcible capturing of women by their supernatural lovers plays so important a part. Then ask yourself the question, Whence came these legends? It is very certain that every effect must have an adequate cause; and it seems that all these stories show a remarkable family resemblance. But the

* II. Peter iii. 4.

Plate 28.   Driven Out.

moment we turn to the Bible record, every difficulty as to their origin vanishes at once. They evidently **all** flow from the terrible **occurrence** narrated in **Genesis, and so** elaborately described in **the** Book of Enoch, when the great leaders of the demon hosts, "**took** themselves wives of all which they chose." The tendency **to keep alive such** stories of intercourse with the gods was sustained by the practice of these abominations, as in the case of the Canaanites. **Strange** to say, no part of the mythologies secures more attention from the average reader than the long and varied accounts of these unions between the gods and their earthly brides, and the feats of strength and other wonders performed by their reputed **sons**, the demigods, like Hercules and his kind. So, in Genesis, the giant offspring were "men of renown."

It is asserted by many that the official marriage **of a** woman to a demon has been performed often in these United States in the last few years. Of course the creature was **not** called a "demon." Oh, no, that would be too bald. He was called a "spirit lover." Do not shake the head and say it is the raving of a lunatic. Remember Enoch and Peter, and Jude, and Moses, and Samuel, and Isaiah, and Paul. "The word of God standeth sure."

Jude used the singular expression that the "filthy dreamers" spoken of by him had "gone in the way of Cain." What did this mean? Only that they had killed people? The remarkable connection seems to point to something more than that. It appears to indicate a sin of a similar nature connected with Cain. The demons and their wives before the flood filled the earth with giant offspring, the "mighty men of renown," whose monumental sins capped the climax of their age. They were all extinguished by the flood, as were all the sinful line of Cain. Strangely persistent efforts have been made by very good men to prove that the Nephilim and Rephaim of the Mosaic period were the descendants of those antediluvian giants. Og, king of Bashan, and the giants of Philistia have been ingeniously traced to supposed ancestors who survived the flood in some way. Job xxvi. 5, is quoted to prove this theory, it being made to read, "Dead things came from under the waters." Here it is is said that the word, translated, "dead things," is the same as the Nephilim or Rephaim spoken of in the wilderness campaigns of Moses and Joshua; and it is argued that this again is similar to the word for "sons of God" of Genesis vi. 2. Of course, all such reasoning flatly denies the express statements of the Word that "every creature in whose nostrils was the breath of life, and every man died." But I see in it a remarkable hidden truth, viz., that the giant offspring of the antediluvian age and the giants of Gath were possibly of the same breed, so to speak. And this being so, I am at no loss whatever to perceive the perfect justice and mercy which decreed the total annihilation of the race whose blood was poisoned throughout with the spawn of demons.

Let those who have charged our God with cruelty in ordering the extermination of innocent babes and helpless women, pause and consider what possible sentence could be passed upon a race every one of which was a veritable germ of disease for soul and body. If it be cruelty to burn up a nest of animals whose entire race are infected with the deadliest typhus fever, then it was cruel to exterminate the seven nations of Canaan Though it be late in the ages, let this vindication of the real *loving mercy* of our gracious and long-suffering God be known by his doubting and "apologetic" children. God regarded his people and knew what was best for them so well that he thoroughly *disinfected* the house in which he placed them. All "germs" have life, but we do not generally stop to think that "antiseptics" are hard on the germs, do we?

In the light of this relevation we can see *why* the Lord would not permit any intermarriages with the heathen nations. Remember that they were expressly told that, "surely they will turn away your heart after their gods." I. Kings xi. 2. God knew that the seed of sin was in the blood, and the result was certain death, moral and spiritual. The severity of the punishment meted out when the man of Israel took the Moabitish princess to his tent, and Phinehas, the son of Aaron thrust them both through with his spear, also at once drops into place as an example of this same "disinfecting" care over his people. And God's special approval of this act of Phinehas is emphasized almost at the end of the sacred canon, when Malachi writes that he "did turn many away from iniquity."* This world was made for a race of men, not of demons; and the only possible way to destroy the disease was to kill all the germs. Hence the flood swept away every man, woman, and child whose life was tainted with the great sin of the age, and the coming flood of fire will do the same.

But those demon leaders were but followers of their greater captain. Satan himself outshone them all with diabolic luster. They were his imitators and servants. Come we then to him, with the clue we have been following, grown most wonderfully as we have pursued the search after the truth. But this requires another chapter.

* Malachi ii. 5, 6.

CHAPTER III.

The Fall of Man.

OUR clew has led us very far back along the lines of history. Past the sins of the Canaanites, and of Israel in Moab; past the sin of the angels, past Enoch, who specially preached against them for their sin, we have come to Satan himself, the old serpent who first deceived our parents in the Garden of Eden. Over all the "wrecks of time" towers this grim and awful personage, against whom Michael the archangel did not dare to bring a railing accusation. In no spirit of lightness, then, I steadily hold on my way when this mighty fallen one stands athwart the track. "The Lord rebuke thee, Satan,"* is the only talisman that gives

* Jude 9.

courage to the heart of man when fighting against such an adversary. But that Lord has promised "to bruise Satan under our feet shortly," and in his strength we will go on.

Who was Satan? To many it will be news to hear that the Bible really tells the answer to this question. At least it is not generally known that his history is written there from the time he was first created till the present. But it is true. Let us examine it.

The reader is of course familiar with the terms "god of this world," "prince of the powers of the air," and "prince of this world." Whence came such titles? How did Satan get to be the "prince of this world?" I answer, by conquest.

He conquered the "Lord of creation," and took his possessions, as all conquerors do. Since that time we know a great deal of his history, but it is of the period before the fall that we now wish to learn. In Ezekiel xxviii. 12-18, is found a most remarkable passage. For some ten verses the Lord has spoken against the "Prince of Tyrus." Tyre and Sidon were the very seat of the foul worship of Astarte, and her frightfully unclean rites and ceremonies. If there was a place on earth where the devil ruled, Tyre was that place. So the man who sat on its throne is called the "Prince," but the devil himself, who controlled that man, is styled in the next verses "the king." Let us read them in full.*

"Son of man, take up a lamentation upon the king of Tyrus, and say unto him, Thus saith the Lord God;

"Thou sealest up the sum, full of wisdom and perfect in beauty. Thou hast been in Eden, the garden of God; every precious stone was thy covering; the sardius, topaz, and the diamond, the beryl, the onyx, and the jasper, the sapphire, the emerald, and the carbuncle, and gold; the workmanship of thy tabrets and of thy pipes was prepared in thee in the day that thou was created. Thou art the annointed cherub that covereth; and I have set thee so; thou wast upon the holy mountain of God; thou hast walked up and down

---

* For a full grasp on the scientific points in this matter, the reader must see "Alpha and Omega," where it is presented in detail.

in the midst of the stones of fire. Thou wast perfect in thy ways from the day that thou wast created till iniquity was found in thee. By the multitude of thy merchandise they have filled the midst of thee with violence, and thou hast sinned; therefore, I will cast thee, as profane, out of the mountain of God; and I will destroy thee, O covering cherub, from the midst of the stones of fire. Thine heart was lifted up because of thy beauty; thou hast corrupted thy wisdom by reason of thy brightness; I will cast thee to the ground; I will lay thee before kings that they may behold thee."

Turn now to Isaiah xiv. and read the doom pronounced upon the king of Babylon, remembering that the ancient mysteries or abominations found their home in Babylon, from whence they passed to Pergamos ("where Satan's seat is." Revelation ii. 13), and thence to Rome, or "Mystery Babylon." (Revelation xvii.)

"Hell from beneath is moved for thee to meet thee at thy coming; it stirreth up the dead for thee, etc. . . . How art thou fallen from heaven, O Lucifer, son of the morning! how art thou cut down to the ground, which did weaken the nations! For thou hast said in thine heart, I will ascend into heaven, I will exalt my throne above the stars of God; I will sit also upon the mount of the congregation, in the sides of the north;* I will ascend above the heights of the clouds; I will be like the Most High. Yet thou shalt be brought down to hell, to the sides of the pit."

The early Christian fathers, Augustine, Tertullian, Ambrose, Jerome, and others were of the opinion that these words of the two great prophets could not refer to any other than Satan himself. Jonathan Edwards said, "Lucifer, before his fall, was the morning star, the covering cherub, the highest and brightest of all creatures." In Luke x. 18, Jesus himself said, "I beheld Satan, as lightning, fall from heaven."

For a thoroughly scientific discussion of Satan, and the language used by Ezekiel, I must refer the reader to my book, " Alpha and Omega, or the

---

* See "Alpha and Omega," page 200.

Birth and **Death** of the World," a book, *after which always this* present work should be read. *A knowledge of the principles therein treated and explained is almost essential to a complete grasp of this present volume.* But for the study before us we will accentuate the main points in the descriptions of the great archangel given by the prophets.

He sealed up the sum of wisdom and perfect beauty. **He** has been in Eden in prehistoric days. **He** was the anointed, covering cherub, specially set so by the Lord. **He** was upon the holy mountain of God. **He** was perfect in all his ways. But iniquity was found in him, because of pride arising from his beauty. **This** pride reached out to ascend above all created things, and finally to be "like the most High." On this account Lucifer (the light bearer) **was cast down to** hell, which "moved" or trembled to meet him at his coming. Truly a wondrously mighty being is here described. And well may he and his work be called "the mystery of iniquity." Against our first parents all his powers were arrayed, for they had succeeded him in the rule of this earth, and every jealous faculty was exerted to the utmost to undo the work of God, and to bring ruin on the new creation. That ruin was accomplished, and the first Adam fell before his great antagonist. Let us now inquire if any further trace of our clew can be discovered in the record of the fall.

The first thing I notice in the experience of Adam and Eve after their sin was a sense of shame connected with the sexual organs of the body. Why was this? Those parts were no less honorable than the others. Why should the secret of life itself have any shame attached to it? There must be found *adequate cause*. There is a reason in all things. God had commanded them to increase and multiply. Why, then, should shame have been located there? Trifling over this will not do. There is a scientific reason as sure as God lives and works by law.

Fig-leaf aprons were made and worn. Again I relentlessly ask, why? Why not dress other parts of the body? Remember that these two beings were utterly unacquainted with the educated proprieties of our experience. They had been absolutely innocent and ignorant of sin, not knowing even what wrong was. All things had been lawful and right to them. They were man and wife, and they were alone. No other human beings saw them. Under the vaporous greenhouse roof of the Edenic age,* they had no need of clothing for comfort, and nobody had told them of its uses nor of any shame. Even God himself asked promptly, "Who told thee that thou wast naked?" And if conscious of nakedness, why did the covering of a small portion of the body satisfy that shame? These questions are perfectly and rigorously logical and reasonable. Effect must have adequate cause. No superstition will answer here, standing as we do at the very portals of the greatest cataclysm the world has ever known.

Notice the words, even in the English. They "knew" they were naked. A little later we read that "Adam *knew* Eve his wife," etc. Why that word? Looking backward through the ages, the Apostle Paul, in consideration again of the vexed question of woman's proper subjection to her hus-

* See "Alpha and Omega."

band, says: "And Adam was not deceived, but the woman was deceived, being in the transgression. *Nevertheless* she shall be saved in *childbearing* if they continue in faith, charity, and holiness with sobriety." I. Timothy ii. 14, 15. Why this special joining of the woman's *transgression* with *childbearing?*

In proper sequence, we thus reach the curse. First came the sentence on the serpent. He had done something very, very evil. "Because thou hast done this," said God, "on thy belly shalt thou go, and dust shalt thou eat." The beautiful creature must henceforth crawl at length, hiding his body in the dust, and, without a hand or paw to assist, must take his food from the earth, soiled and covered with whatever came in contact with it. But see! "And I will put enmity between thee and the woman, and between thy seed and her seed; it shall bruise thy head, and thou shalt bruise his heel." Why between the serpent and the "woman"? Had not Adam also fallen? Why this coupling of the "seed" of the woman with the working out of the curse?

These are profound questions. Ponder them deeply.

Then to the woman: "I will greatly multiply thy sorrow and thy conception." Why was this selected? Did God arbitrarily pick out this bodily function for the operation of the curse? Or was there some reasonable connection? I insist that *God has a reason for everything he does, and that that reason is always strictly and truly scientific.* "In sorrow thou shalt bring forth children." Here the same questions are pertinent. But now comes a matter of tremendous import. "Thy desire shall be to thy husband, and he shall bear rule over thee."

Ah! what does this mean? Here we have the startling difference between the human species and the brute creation. And again I press the searching query, why the joining of the curse to the desire subjected to the husband? No other appetite is so bound. The female among the brutes is not so "subject." Just the reverse. The male follows her in the matter of desire. At the risk of seeming repetitious, I say again, every effect must have an adequate cause. (And I assert here that such cause can be found alone in the fact that the sin was connected with the sexual appetite in some way.) God is a God of reason. The "desire" was all right. God's special selection of the marriage figure all through the Bible shows how perfectly pure and holy it can be, when it is as he made it. God had commanded them to multiply, but they had not yet done so. Why?

Another vital point has now been reached. The brute creation answers the last question. Their "season" had not come. "To the word and the testimony" and you will find this proved beyond a peradventure. The very language of the curse clearly declares a reversal of conditions. And, if the curse inaugurated a reversal, then before the curse things were otherwise. Is this not undeniable? But the curse said to the woman, "thy desire shall be to thy husband." Then, by all the rules of sense and logic, before the curse her desire was not to her husband, but was independent, as in the case of the animals. Therefore woman, before the fall, had a "season" like the rest of the animal world. If there be any flaw in that logic, let it be pointed out.

John says, "Cain was of that wicked one, and slew his brother." He also wrote the words, "Beloved, we are of God, and the whole world lieth in the wicked one." Jesus said to the Pharisees, "Ye are of your father, the Devil [Diabolus] and the lusts of your father ye do." Will this help us to understand why Jude says the "filthy dreamers" who had crept into the church, had "gone in the way of Cain?"

CHAPTER IV.

What is the "Carnal Mind."*

SATAN is an angel. Angels are invariably represented as male. There is a great deal of unsupported theory abroad concerning a dual nature in the angels, seeking to base itself upon the words of Jesus, "In the resurrection they neither marry nor are given in marriage, but are as the angels." But this bare statement of the Lord is wholly without explanatory passages, and we can make nothing certain out of it. Meanwhile we are very sure that all the angels mentioned in the Bible are classed as masculine.

Satan hated man, and left no stone unturned in his search for some way to accomplish his over-

* A chapter for the special study of theologians.

WHAT IS THE "CARNAL MIND." 295

throw. In trying the weak points in man's armor he was guided by a previous study of the brute creation which had antedated man's arrival upon the scene. (Here the archangel had observed the power of the physical appetites, and could not fail to see that the sexual appetite was the strongest.

There was no use in wasting time looking for something wrong for man to do, for all things were his, and all things were lawful. Satan knew full well that the only possible way for a perfect being to sin* was to use some right thing in a wrong way or at a wrong time. He also knew that a temptation was no temptation unless it appealed to some desire strongly felt by the tempted one. He had nothing to offer Adam, for Adam already owned all that there was. He had himself sinned by the undue working of pride because of his own transcendent beauty. But being acquainted with evil, he probably regarded that manner of temptation as too slow, or as inferior to an appeal to a strong natural desire. This is proven by the temptation of the second Adam.

* **Except by** originating pride, as Lucifer himself had done.

Hungry from his forty days' fast, he was solicited to make bread to satisfy his hunger. Of course the natural and proper feeling of hunger responded to the suggestion, and undoubtedly Christ felt hungrier. A little later he made bread enough to feed five thousand men; but then He refused. Why? Simply because it would have been sin to have done so at the suggestion of Satan, when that suggestion was poisoned by the doubt, " If thou be the Son of God." That was the way Satan approached Eve, with a doubt of God's word: "Yea, hath God said?" Are you sure He meant what He said? The way in which all " higher criticism" invariably begins.

Beyond controversy the second Adam stood, exactly where the first Adam fell. But the temptation of the former was addressed to a proper physical appetite, and pointed with a doubt. Therefore the temptation of the latter must have been addressed to a physical appetite also. We know it was pointed with a doubt, so the analogy is perfect. But some one will object that the appetite addressed in the case of Eve was that of hunger, and not the sexual. I answer that such a thought is absolutely barred out of the premises. It is impossible that Adam and Eve were ever violently hungry. Perhaps you never thought of that, but it must be true. Remember that they were physically immortal; that is they knew no decay of tissue at the time of the temptation. They had not begun to die, because the evil actinism of the solar ray had not penetrated the overhanging vapors,* and consequently had not known decay. It is therefore certain that they could not know hunger in the imperious sense. Hence the appeal to this appetite could not be expected to meet with much response. The element of pride was undoubtedly included; but this cannot be the only thing involved on account of the parallelism between the temptation and that of the Saviour. His was certainly physical. Then so was Eve's. She had no reason to fast forty days as Jesus did, so there is absolutely no room for the supposition that hunger was the basis of the appeal in her case. The element of pride, which I have allowed,

* See "Alpha and Omega."

could not have been very strong; and the same may be said of the mere desire for extra knowledge. We cannot imagine that this was anything more than a curious wish. I insist that temptation must meet with some strong response to have any power whatever. And it is plain that Satan would not select a strong point to attack when a weaker was ready to his hand. His nature has certainly changed very much in six thousand years if he ever did such a thing.

As has been remarked, Satan had had plenty of time to see the working of the sexual appetite in the case of the animals; for they had been increasing and multiplying for a long time before man appeared upon the scene. (But now a female comes to Adam; and as the female always leads the male in the sex relation, in the animal creation, Satan shrewdly guessed that through this appetite was the most likely road to success, especially if he could secure the co-operation of the female.) Remember, the real object of attack was Adam, and not Eve. No matter whether our sisters like it or not, the fact is absolutely beyond dispute, man was the head of creation, and woman was but a "help suitable for him." There cannot be a particle of doubt that if Adam had resisted the temptation offered him by his wife, she would have perished, and probably another "helpmeet" been found. Certainly the creation would not have shared her fate, it would have stood with Adam. Satan knew this perfectly, and therefore, like the skillful general he is, made an indirect attack, adopting the tactics of seeking to obtain an ally in the camp. And in this he succeeded, only too well.

God's command to "increase and multiply" had not as yet been obeyed. Reason will be sought in vain outside of the fact that Eve's "season" had not come around.* Watching its approach, Satan drew near, and tempted her slightly in advance. Remember the temptation to the second Adam was to gratify a normal, proper appetite in advance of the proper time and means; and also remember

---

* For the scientific discussion as to why it had not come, see "Alpha and Omega." It may be said here, however, that seed forming probably depends upon the operation of decay, and, of course, decay had not begun until just before the time of the scene in Eden.

that thus only can a perfect being be solicited to sin. It probably never occurred to you that Eve could not possibly *know* all about the forbidden tree and its fruit. But she certainly could not. Sin is an experience; that is, the knowledge of sin is. Unfallen angels know nothing of sin. They see and deplore its effects, but they do not *know* it. So Satan told the truth when he said, "Ye shall know good and evil." They only knew good. They knew absolutely nothing of evil. God had said they must not know this very thing. "The tree of the knowledge of good and evil!" They did know the good — the first half; but they did not know the "evil" — the second half. Therefore, what they were forbidden was the knowledge of evil, or the distinction and difference between the two. As they knew nothing whatever about evil, it was impossible that this suggestion could have any soliciting power unless it entered the mind reinforced by the appeal of a powerful appetite in a state of excitement. Surely this is beyond dispute.

Hence I conclude that Satan found our first

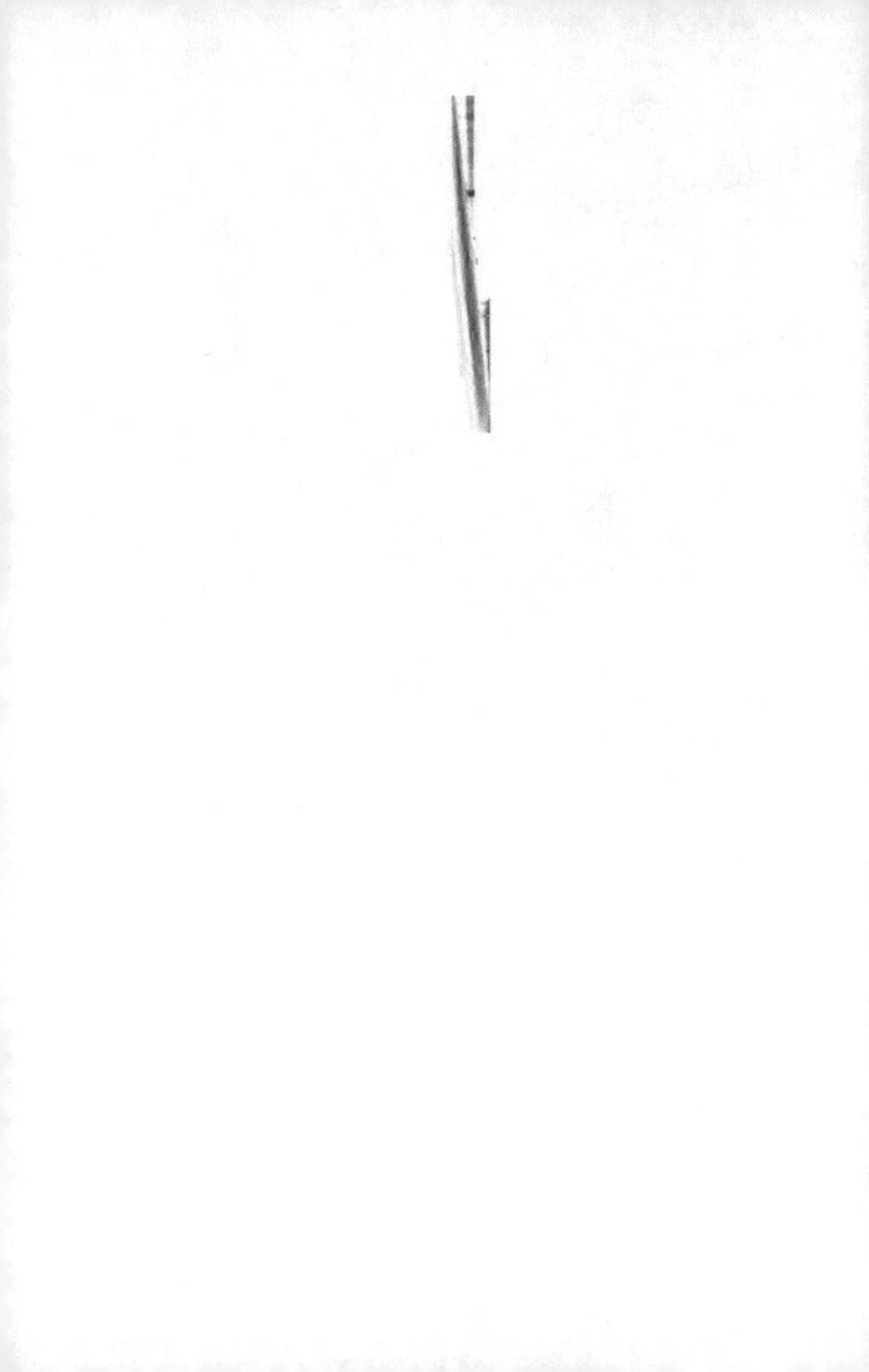

WHAT IS THE "CARNAL MIND." 303

mother in the rising fever of her first "season," and seized the opportunity to tempt her to indulgence with himself. He could not take her by force, as his lieutenants did the wicked daughters of the apostate race, just before the flood. Her will must be captured. So the temptation was gradual, and disguised under the promise of benefit of "deep knowledge of mysteries." (How like his mode of approach to-day.) Very likely unnatural excitation was used to urge the organism, unaccustomed to the spur of unbalanced conditions, to the desirable state.* In this, the will of the tempted woman took part, and thus the surrender was complete. What is impossible for the instinct-guarded brute, is all too possible for the reasoning human, and the battle was won. (Satan cohabited with Eve, teaching her how to secure pleasure when the natural time had not fully come.) (And this knowledge, and this practice she communicated to her husband.) Tradition has always held that Adam partook of the fruit through his in-

---

* Thus originating that terrible evil that curses so large a part of the race, — the habit of self abuse, the appalling effects of which are so well known to medical men.

tense love for his wife; that rather than submit to final separation, he chose to share her fall. I opine that this tradition has more truth than has been supposed, but in a different form from the common idea. Through the tremendous pull of the sexual appetite, aroused by the excited state of the woman, he also felt the power of a solicitation addressed to a strong natural desire, and yielded, just as she had done.

I call the scientific mind to consider that it was not possible for Adam to be tempted before Eve on this line. He had no season. Males never do. In his perfectly balanced physical condition, free from all trace or taint of the diseased appetites we inherit, he knew no special desire until it was aroused in the way God had intended, viz., by the presence of desire in the woman. Hence, the only way to approach the pair through this strongest appetite implanted in their constitutions, was to go to the woman first, and through her to solicit the man. Thus, she who was made to be a helpmeet for the man, by this strategem of the arch adversary, became first the helpmeet of Satan. (Perhaps it is not altogether fanciful to see in the old feudal custom for the lord of the manor to take to his bed on her marriage night every girl in his domain, before she was given to her husband, a suggestion of the original victory of the father of all "fleshly lusts that war against the soul.")

But I bring forward another analogy. This function was the one appointed by the Creator to propagate the species. (So Satan selected it as that through which to destroy the race.) God said it was to be used to perpetuate life. Satan twisted it into the means of perpetuating death. The very thing God had made to give life through a seed, was turned to hand down death through the same. Hence Satan and his hosts rejoiced, for God seemed to be defeated at the very outset. But right here comes in the real force of the primal promise, ("The seed of the woman shall bruise the serpent's head.") The very thing which Satan was congratulating himself had been turned to his perpetual victory was to be the means of bringing about his final destruction. He thought he had everlastingly poisoned the seed at its fountainhead, and that scientifically it never could be any better. But God steps in and declares that even that scientific impossibility is not impossible with the Almighty, but that on the contrary, the very seed should be the agent to overcome the victor of Eden. Truly, God "maketh the wrath of man to praise him; and the remainder of wrath he doth restrain." Our God is he who can and does wrest the most perfect victory out of the very jaws of utter defeat. And He seems to take pleasure in showing His infinite power by using the most important elements of the failure to constitute the success.

I said Satan supposed he had poisoned the seed at the fountainhead, and that it never could be any better. This calls up a very important point. Many breeders of stock declare that the first offspring of a female seems to impart its quality to all that may come after. For example, they claim that if a mare be served to an ass, and bear a mule foal, and then afterward be served to a horse, and bear horse colts, the latter will always show a streak of mule in them. Some probably oppose this conclusion, but the belief in it is widespread. The thought suggested is this: After the fall, we read that, "Adam knew Eve, his wife, and she conceived and bare Cain, and said I have gotten a man from the Lord." But she was fallen and blinded by sin. Cain was not from the Lord at all, but from Satan. John says, "Cain was of that evil one." Whether Cain was the actual progeny of Satan, or whether he was merely the recipient of the full force of the poisonous seed of the adversary, is not a matter for dogmatism. I strongly incline to the belief that he was the actual son of Satan. Certain is it that he "was of that wicked one." The word of the Lord is foundation enough for me. I know no court of appeal after "Thus saith the Lord." It may be that the seed was not actually energized until Adam "knew his wife"; but I see no reason to conclude thus when it is certain that centuries later the angels had offspring by the women of the time.* They were simply imita-

---

* On this point, see my "Alpha and Omega" in relation to the matter of producing seed before the fall. As the actual ripening and bearing of seed in plant or animal seems to have been slow under the dim

tors of their great leader. (At all events, the firstborn child was infected by the seed of the devil.

And therefore, in perfect scientific causation, every subsequent child of the race has been infected also. The "streak of the mule" is in all the sons of men.

Do not laugh at this; it is too serious a matter. *Effects must have a cause.* Here is the sinful nature. It is certainly transmitted from father to son. But how? The truth is always perfectly scientific. Only our bungling attempts to explain things from wrong premises are not so. The moment we find the proper key, all the wards of the most complicated lock drop into place, and the door swings wide open. "Everything is easy when you know how," as the boys say.

---

light of the previous ages, so it is thinkable that in the case of Eve, under the perfectly balanced environment of the Edenic period, the conception from Satan was not developed until the change of climate that followed, and the entrance of decay, together with the excitation of intercourse with Adam, brought about that development. Before this, she had been like the trees of Genesis i. 2., "whose seed was in itself." The germ had simply slumbered. The resurrection will bring the time when marriage ceases. There is a thought here. Will the seed be "in itself" once more in that complete life?

Why did God lay so much stress upon the consecration to Him of "all that openeth the matrix?" Why did he say, "All the first-born of thy sons thou shalt redeem?" (Exodus xxxiv. 20.) Who will say, in the light of these solemn facts, that this was not a type of the principle we are discussing? Why redeem the firstborn? Because the state of the firstborn bespeaks the same state for all subsequent births. God meant to write the story of redemption everywhere. And He has done it. In letters of inflexible science I see it written in these laws of Moses, and trace the perfect analogies back to the first great promise of the seed who was to be and has become the "Firstborn from the dead." He was "redeemed with a Lamb," even with himself, the Lamb of God. And thus He bespeaks the same glorious state for us, who, by the power of grace divine, are "born again of water and of the Spirit."

What tremendous import can be seen in the "figure" of the "new birth!" In this heaven-sent light, it ceases to be a "figure," and blazes before our astonished eyes as a reality, a scientific fact. (We were "conceived in sin" sure enough) No figure about it. And we "must be born again" actually and positively, and be born redeemed at that — redeemed by the Lamb that was slain to be our propitiation. Even as in us the spirit of evil has conceived the sin, so the Holy Spirit must bring forth the divine life within us, and "Christ *be formed in us* — the hope of glory."

Types are all very well, but stop long enough to think that there cannot be a type without the thing typified. You must have the literal, or the spiritual can have no tangible existence. Figures cannot be made from nothing. Shadows do not cast themselves. God said, "Sanctify unto me all the firstborn; whatsoever openeth the womb among the children of Israel, both of man and of beast, it is mine."* "Behold, I have taken the Levites from among the children of Israel instead of all the firstborn that openeth the matrix among the children of Israel; therefore, the Levites shall be

* Exodus xiii. 2.

mine; because all the firstborn are mine; for, on the day that I smote all the firstborn in the land of Egypt, I hallowed unto me all the firstborn in Israel, both man and beast; mine shall they be; I am the Lord."* "The firstborn of man shalt thou surely redeem, and the firstborn of unclean beasts shalt thou redeem."†

All Bible students agree that Pharoah was a type of the "prince of this world." In smiting his firstborn, and the firstborn of all his people, God typically declared the **fate** of the "seed of the adversary." And in redeeming all the firstborn of Israel, he as plainly declared the scheme of salvation to the race. Cain, the firstborn of sin, killed his brother. Christ, the "firstborn of God," saves his brothers. God neglects no analogy, parallel, or type. All is perfectly harmonious, wherever we turn. The Levites — the priests — were taken instead of the firstborn of Israel. So Christ — the priest after the order of Melchisedek — is taken for us all. The clean beasts (cow, sheep, and goat) were not redeemed.

* Numbers iii. 12, 13.   † Numbers xviii. 15.

So clean men, were there any such, need no redemption. "Christ came not to call the righteous, but sinners to repentance," and "to seek and save the lost" only.

Eve thought her firstborn was "from the Lord." Multitudes of her descendants have made the mistake of supposing that the carnal mind, the firstborn nature in us, is from the Lord; that we are so created of God, and cannot get rid of this incubus until death. I think that there is no objection to this, always provided that we are correct in our definition of the "carnal mind." It is the purpose of this chapter to give a new definition, and one which I believe will at once remove most of the endless debates on this disputed subject from the field of polemics. I have long been of the opinion that there is a widespread confusion of ideas on this topic; and of late have arrived at the conclusion that very much of the fighting has been about things differently understood by the combatants. Being in the front rank of this controversy for over a dozen years, I feel qualified to

WHAT IS THE "CARNAL MIND." 315

speak with knowledge, if **not** with authority. **Let us essay a primary definition.**

(The "carnal mind" is the fallen, sinful disposition, or tendency in man.)

I think **no** one will object **to** this. But just here I call attention to the fact that this disposition, **or tendency,** resides in two distinct places —the will, and the physical inclinations **or appetites.** Here is the great point that **is almost entirely overlooked** in the discussions on this subject; and just here is the key **to a reasonable solution** of the difficulty. This "carnal mind" **is the** actual poison of the serpent; it is Satan's seed in the captured race, scientifically transmitted. But remember, it is in two places. It is not all in the will, nor is it all in the physical body. It resides in both. **We are** spiritually *dead* in sin, and **mentally** and physically dying from the poison infused by the serpent *

But faith in Jesus is exercised; faith in "the seed of the woman who has bruised the serpent's

---

* **Our environment** of course plays an important part in the physical **decay.** For this see "Alpha and Omega."

head;" and the spiritual part is created new; it is "born again, of water and of the Spirit," and "redeemed by a Lamb"—the Lamb of God. Yet the "carnal mind" remains, and "the flesh lusteth against the spirit, and the spirit against the flesh," more or less, as temptation's waves rise and fall about the soul.

In this dilemma the command of God sounds out from Old and New Testaments to press on into Canaan, to destroy the Amalekitish "flesh," to be "sanctified wholly," and directs us to bring this about by "presenting our bodies a living sacrifice unto God," remembering that "the altar sanctifieth the gift." The sentence of death and total crucifixion and removal stands against the "old man," and he is to be "put off" just as positively and as literally as "his deeds." And as all things are received by faith we are exhorted to "reckon ourselves to be dead indeed [not make believe] unto sin, but alive unto God, through Jesus Christ our Lord."*

Just here the split has occurred between the

---

* Romans vi. 11.

WHAT IS THE "CARNAL MIND." 317

two important schools. Feeling the presence in the body of the tendency towards indulgence, the one division contend that this reckoning is not a real death, but only a reckoning, i. e., a making believe. But the other side stoutly maintain that the death is real, that it is "dead indeed," as the text plainly declares. And at this disputed point I hope to present a satisfactory solution that will be apprehended as reasonable by both sides.

We all agree that nothing but an actual death will get us rid of "sin in the flesh." The sinning part or principle must die. The law is absolutely inexorable. "The soul that sinneth, it shall die." There is no escape, and no other remedy. The only way to get rid of germs, is to burn them up. Now, remembering that the carnal mind resides in the will, as well as the body, I think we can agree that, by the grace and power of God the *will* may be set free entirely from its poison. Certainly a man, who has been "born again," can come to the point of presenting himself, with all his plans and purposes, his likes and dislikes, his possessions and his reputation, in one final offering on God's altar. In other words, he can consecrate his whole will to God. And beyond doubt, God stands ready to accept such an offering, and "sanctify it wholly" by the blood of the everlasting covenant, applied by the Spirit of Grace. This done, and the work of the Holy Ghost received by faith ("sanctified by the faith that is in me") what has become of the carnal mind, at least so far as the will is concerned? It is certainly burned up by the fire of the Holy Ghost, and the heart is made "pure."

But I submit that this sanctification has not removed the poisoned, fallen tendency from the physical body. Here is a vital distinction, the neglecting of which has led to the bulk of the dispute. The appetite for food in a sanctified Christian, still has to be watched, or it will incline towards undue gratification. And so with every appetite we possess. These appetites are blind; they are unreasoning; they are instinctive. And being fallen, being thoroughly off their balance since the fall, and *while the present environ-*

ment *prevails*,* they constantly tend towards excess. Now what remedy is at hand?

On this Paul speaks, "I keep under my body, and bring it into subjection."† Who is the "I" that keeps it under? Evidently the will. And to what is the body brought into subjection? To the same. When Paul was sanctified, and his heart was "purified by faith" the carnality was destroyed (Romans vi. 6) from his will, but not from his physical flesh. Grasp this distinction fully. It is of absolute importance. And for this perfect riddance in the body, Paul, and the "whole creation groaned and travailed."

On this part of the subject those who advocate the "two natures" are right. We cannot get rid of the carnality, or unbalance in the physical flesh until the resurrection, when this "vile body" (body of low estate) will be changed. The evil of anticipating the Millennium, of which I have spoken, has perhaps to some extent influenced the more extreme advocates of "holiness" on this point. But we can, and must get rid of carnality in the

---

* See "Alpha and Omega."   † 1. Corinthians ix. 27.

will in this life. The present "will of God" is "our sanctification," and if our wills refuse to meet his will, we of course remain unsanctified.

The beast does not have to keep the body under. His instinct manages that for him, because his nature is not fallen as is ours. He shares in the death (physical) of the age, as did men who had not the law (Romans v. 14), but knows no sin. But our bodies are actually and scientifically tainted and poisoned with sin, and unbalanced in all their functions, and this continues after the spirit is sanctified wholly, requiring to be rigidly kept under by the will all the days of our life.

No wholly sanctified woman has a season for her sexual appetite. Things continue as they were in this matter. This at once answers the much-mooted question as to how the child of wholly sanctified parents can have a carnal mind like the child of unsaved sinners. Remember that the new birth of the spirit is an original creation each time it takes place. It is not and cannot be transmitted by natural generation, for it is not natural in any sense of that word. But the carnality is natural, and is subject to the rigorous laws of physical transmission expressed by the original enactment, "after his kind." The will — the spirit — of the wholly sanctified parents is perfectly pure as they "walk in the light" and are kept clean by the blood. But the physical body is not pure, as Adam's was; and *will not be till the resurrection.* That is the very thing that is reserved for that greatest future day. "To be clothed upon!"* How it excited the longing of the Apostle. And how we all reach out for it. But let us not anticipate. A baby is born innocent, but not balanced. It is born savable, but not saved. There is no new heart in it. As it grows the unbalance prevails, sin rests in it, and it "must be born again."

On this point I am afraid that many who advocate "Divine healing" are overstepping the truth. God heals the sick — I *know* it, for my heart disease that defied all medical aid for seven long years cannot now be even traced by the most skillful physician. But God does not run ahead

* II. Corinthians v. 2.

of his own laws and his own express declarations. While we are in the bodily flesh we retain our physical unbalance. No use for any son of man to claim otherwise. Our appetites and passions must be kept continually under (in their proper place and time, which they all have) by the sanctified will. And for this God always supplies the power, as we look to him. The "whole spirit, soul, and body may be preserved *blameless*," for blame is only imputed where there is law, and at present there is no law or means provided for a perfect body; but we are only to be presented "faultless" on the resurrection day.*

The sexual appetite is the one which specially concerns the propagation of the species, hence it affects all the other appetites of the body. The poison is there, and cannot be taken out but by the death of the organism. "Except a corn of wheat fall into the ground and *die*, it remaineth alone." In the moment of death God steps in and works the miracle of life, fresh from his hand. In the spirit this is done now. In the body it will

---

* See Jude 24, and I. Thessalonians v. 23.

be done at the resurrection. **When** the soul is ready **to die to** self, God makes the thing real, **and destroys the** " **body of sin** " by the fiery breath **of the spirit.** But this death has to precede the life, be it by but a moment of time. Just so the physical body must die to its old life before it can be " clothed upon" with immortality, and, " this mortal will **put on immortality**" "in a moment, in the twinkling of an eye," **but it must** be after the necessary death.

Thus it is that God breaks the power of death, and **destroys** its sting. Death itself is actually made, in a sense, the portal of life. At least it is **the necessary antecedent** condition. **It is not a** *friend; it is never the sanctifier;* no, no! God sanctifies the soul now **through** faith, and gives the " **earnest of our** inheritance." And he holds out the promise that the " groaning creation " shall soon be satisfied, **when at the** resurrection, we " awake in his likeness." **Then** "death, the last enemy, shall be destroyed," but not till then. Thus Paul declares it, "Then shall be brought to pass **the saying that is** written, Death is swallowed up in victory." When is this to be? "When this corruptible has put on incorruption, and this mortal has put on immortality."

There is another point of the greatest importance. "Sin is not imputed where there is no law."* That is, God does not hold us responsibly guilty for being in a state which we cannot help, and out of which he has made no present mode of escape. If there be no such thing as what Paul calls "sanctified wholly" possible to us, then we are not guilty or to blame because we are not sanctified wholly. If it be impossible for any man to have all sin cleansed from his heart (or will) in this life, then nobody is to blame for having sin in the heart. If God has made no law for the special case, then that case goes free. That is all there is about it. It is astonishing that such a simple axiomatic truth should not be apprehended without argument. We are not to blame for having a carnal mind, for we were born so, without being consulted in the matter. We were simply put here with the tendency in us. The instinct

* Romans v. 13.

of common justice **tells every** man he cannot be held responsible **for his own** height, or **color, or** natural gifts. **The man who** has two **talents is not expected to make five.** The born cripple **is not asked to race with the perfect** athlete. **So God holds** no man responsible **for Adam's sin, and no man was ever** damned for what he absolutely **could not** help. **The reverse** inference in manmade theologies has manufactured a great many infidels. No man is guilty because he **does not make a new heart in himself. He cannot do it. No use to try.**

But we are responsible **for the use we** have **made of** the "way **of escape"** God has provided. The new heart is offered **to** us freely. Will we accept? (If not we die in our sins, **not Adam's.***) In precisely **the same** manner the question of the **"carnal mind"** must be treated **if** we wish to avoid hopeless confusion and inconsistency. We cannot **help** having it, nor can **we rid** ourselves of it. **But** God "requires us to love Him with all our **heart"** (not with a part). If we are unable to do

* John viii. 24.

so, and if God has provided no present means, *then the command is a farce and its disobedience a necessity.* But to make sin a necessity, is to make it no sin at all; not in any responsible sense. It may be uncleanness, viewed from the absolute standpoint; but there is no responsibility, or personal guilt attached. Black is black; it can never be white or blue or gray; but the African carries not the smallest particle of guilt on account of his color. Notwithstanding he *is* black, and only a miracle can make him white.

What then can we do? Avail ourselves of the " way of escape " that has been provided. God promised ages ago, " And the Lord thy God will circumcise thy heart, and the heart of thy seed, to love the Lord thy God with all thy heart, and with all thy soul (not when you die, but) that thou mayst live." Deuteronomy xxx. 6. " And I will put my spirit within you, and cause you to walk in my statutes, and ye shall keep my judgments and do them." Ezekiel xxxvi. 27. If then we " reckon ourselves also to be dead indeed unto sin, and alive unto God through Jesus

Plate 34.   Serpents of Remorse.

Christ our Lord," the Lord accepts the sacrifice on the altar; the "altar sanctifieth the gift," and the Holy Ghost comes in fire to make his abode in the soul. The will is set free from self, and wholly given to God. Certainly this will not be disputed by anyone.

But the body still contains the seeds of death and of decay. The state of unbalance, the tendency towards indulgence, the carnal mind in the literal flesh, still remains. It is not worth while debating with the exceptional fanatic who would contend otherwise. Perfect deliverance on this point is distinctly reserved to the glad day of the resurrection. But I call attention to the fact that *this very reservation at once removes all personal responsibility for, and guilt on account of, the continued presence of the unbalance or carnality in the literal physical flesh.* It is certainly unbalanced. It is surely "unclean" from the absolute standpoint of the Almighty. But we cannot help that. We are black, but not guilty or responsible, because at present there has been made no "way of escape." I beg of my critical readers to let this sink deep into their minds.

"Where there is no law there is no sin."* God hath said it. And it is certain that at present there is no "law" for the removal of this carnal weakness, or tendency from our physical flesh. But there is a law for continually keeping it under, that is, absolutely denying it any excess, or any violation of the proper place or time. Therefore there is no sin in its presence, at least so far as our responsibility is concerned. "It is appointed unto all men once to die." Hence, "death worketh in us." Decay goes right on while this present environment lasts.† But "sin is not imputed"; and therefore, as all sin is cleansed from the heart or will by the precious blood of Christ, his perfect righteousness (even in the physical body) is accepted in our stead, and God is "well pleased." Thus he was "pleased" with Enoch. Thus he called Job and Noah "perfect."

In the spirit,—the heart or will,—the death to self is actual. All sin is cast out when the in-

* Romans iv. 15.   † See "Alpha and Omega," Note viii.

WHAT IS THE "CARNAL MIND." 333

dividual experiences his Pentecost. There is no sin on the heart, and there is no sin in the heart either. But in the case of the body things are different. The death to sin there is merely "reckoned." It is not yet actual,—not till the resurrection. There is no sin on the body, but there is sin (strictly) in the body. The first work—in the spirit—is a positive work, holiness is actually and directly imparted by the Holy Ghost. The second—in the physical body—is not a positive work, holiness is imputed by the Spirit of truth.

One great mistake made by earnest Christians is to whip themselves because of the mere presence of the bodily appetites and passions. They think they cannot be holy unless they are dead to the natural motions of the physical flesh. And a host of teachers and preachers have never clearly seen this necessary distinction between the flesh— the carnal mind in the heart, and the flesh—the physical organism. (Remember that every appetite and propensity of the natural body is made of God. It is not a sin to have it at all.) It is eminently right and proper that it should be there.

Monks and nuns are made from the wrong view of this subject. Sin arises only when one of these proper appetites is allowed to step out of its right place, — when it is not kept under. It has a place, but that place is under the will, which, when sanctified, always says "Yes" to the will of God. "To everything there is a season, and a time to every purpose under heaven." But when we let them out of their "season" or "time" it becomes sin. I conclude, therefore, —

1. That the carnal mind is the seed of Satan, transmitted through the race from our first parents under the inflexible law, "after his kind."

2. That after regeneration (conversion) this carnal mind remains in the heart and in the body, unaffected as to its inherent character, and incapable of improvement, being always under sentence of death, and that death is the only possible means of its removal.

3. That at the time that the believer apprehends and receives Christ as his sanctification and is baptized with the Holy Ghost, and with fire, this sentence is carried out literally and actually

in the heart (or will), and the old man is put off, as well as his deeds; the "body of sin being destroyed" from the heart.

4. That the carnal tendency to blind and unreasoning or instinctive indulgence in any and all of the appetites, desires, and ambitions of the physical flesh, still remains, and continues to remain in the holiest saints until the resurrection (practically, in this age, till they die).

5. That while we live the rule of our being is to "keep under the (physical) body, and bring it into subjection" to the sanctified will, which will has been given up wholly to God. We must watch every day against the temptations to excess or neglect, which are so easily and naturally fallen into; and, if we so "watch and pray" we will find that God, "with the temptation always provides a way of escape that we may be able to bear it."

6. That in this blessed realization of salvation we have both state and standing in Christ perfect and assured. Our standing is always and only in Him. And our state is without sin either in or on the heart, and without sin on the body; but

with sin (from God's absolute standard) in the body, till we die, or the resurrection day comes.

7. That the holiness of Christ is imparted to our spirits by the Holy Ghost, thus fulfilling the command, "Be ye *yourselves* also holy" (R. V.); but that this holiness is imputed to the physical body at present. The body is yet carnal, but "sin is not imputed," because there is now no law prescribing a way of escape. Nevertheless we groan, looking for the "redemption of the body."

I am persuaded that a clear apprehension of these simple distinctions will remove a great many clouds from the theological sky, and raise a flag of truce on many a battlefield. Search the Scriptures with the aid of scientific logic, and see if these things be not so

CHAPTER V.

The Cross and Phallic Worship.

UNDER the head of "Phallic Worship" the American Encyclopedia gives the following: —

"Phallic Worship, the adoration of the generative organs as symbols of the creative power of nature. In early ages the sexual emblems were adored as most sacred objects, and in the several polytheistic systems the act or principle of which the phallus was the type was represented by a deity to whom it was consecrated; in Egypt by Khem, in India by Siva, in Assyria by Pul, in primitive Greece by Pan, and later by Priapus, in Italy by Mutinus or Priapus, among the Teutonic and Scandinavian nations by Fricco, and in Spain by Hortanes. Phallic monuments and sculptured emblems are found in all parts of the world. In the cave temples of Elephanta, Salsette, and Ellora, and other sanctuaries of Siva, the *lingham* or phallus, frequently in conjunction with the *yohni* or *cteis* (the symbol of the female organ), its counterpart, is everywhere prominent. In Egypt it is sculptured on the walls of the temples, or erected as obelisks before them. The *crux ansata*,* so common on Egyptian monuments, symbolizes the union of the active and passive principles of nature. In the Etruscan tombs have been found crosses formed of four phalli. The two obelisks before the temple of Hieropolis represented phalli, as did many of the stone pillars of whose erection we have historic record. The columns set up by Sesostris to commemorate his victories are said to have borne phallic emblems.

"The Spanish conquerors of America found phallic symbols in Mexico, Central America, and Peru. In Panuco the phallus was adored in the temples, and in Tlascala were worshipped both the

*See Plate 37.

Plate 35. MISERY IN COMPANIONSHIP.

phallus and the cteis In the court of the grand temple of **Cuzco**, and in front of the temples of **Yucatan**, stood phallic pillars; and many monuments, the object of whose building is lost in antiquity, such as the Round Towers of Ireland, the Druidical stones, etc., are believed by some to have a similar significance. Phallic processions and observances are said by Herodotus to have been introduced from Egypt into Greece by Melampus. In the former country the phallus of the bull Apis was carried in procession during the festivals of Osiris by women, to the music of flutes. In Greece the emblem was used in the festivals of **Bacchus, Aphrodite,** Demeter, **and Apollo,** and was borne openly in processions by bearers called *phallophspoi*, to the music of phallic songs. According to Saint Augustine the phallus was consecrated in **Rome** in the temples of Liber, and the cteis in **those** of Libera. At the festivals of Venus the Roman matrons adored the emblem in her temple on **the Quirinal, and bore it** thence **with great** pomp to the sanctuary of Venus Erycina, **outside** the Colline gate, where it was presented to the statue of the goddess and then returned to the former place. In the spring the Roman rustics carried the phallus across the fields, to insure fertility. (These processions were finally suppressed by the Roman senate on account of the immorality which sprung from them.)

"A secondary point was the use of the emblem as a *fascinum* or charm against evil influences. With this object it was put over gateways and doors, just as the horseshoe is by the superstitious of the present day, and hung around the necks of children as a preventive against witchcraft. It was also worn by barren women with the belief that it would conduce to fruitfulness. For a like purpose votive offerings of phalli were often made in the temples. (Great numbers of small ones in bronze and porcelain have been found at Herculaneum and Pompeii and in the Egyptian tombs.) In the ninth century the use of the phallus as an amulet or charm was so general that it was anathematized by the church, and the anathema was repeated in the thirteenth and fourteenth centuries; but to this day, in some parts of Italy, the peasants still hang the emblem on the necks of their infants to protect them from the evil eye.

"Phallic worship still prevails in the east. In **the temples of Siva the phallus,** crowned with flowers and surmounted by a golden star, **is exposed in the** sanctuary, and lamps are kept burning **before it.** The devotees of Siva wear small images of the emblem, **made of** gold, ivory, **or** crystal, **as ornaments, and they** are often buried with them. Offerings of phalli **are still made in** the Buddhist temples of China by barren women, just as they were by Roman wives in the temples of Venus."*

Another authority says: "The phallus was **the** representation **of the** male organ of generation, **and was used in the** Dionysian festivals of ancient Greece as the emblem of the power of procreation. It was the object **of** common worship through the nature religions **of the east,** and was called by many names, as *linga, joni, pollear,* etc. Originally no other meaning was attached to it than the

---

* At the present time this emblem is in use among the Theosophists. Recently, in lecturing in San Francisco, Mrs. Annie Besant wore one upon her breast. It came from India, and was of great age.

allegorical one of the mysterious union between the male and female, which seems to be the reason for the continuance of the animate creation, but later its worship became so vile as to be put down by the Roman senate on account of the fearful immorality to which it gave rise.

The Phœnicians trace its origin to the worship of Adonis, Egypt to Osiris, Phrygians to Attys, and Greeks to Dionysus. All contain the myth of the god deprived of the powers of procreation, and slain by Typhon, the serpent deity. Readers of my work, "Alpha and Omega, or The Birth and Death of the World," will see here the truth of the shutting out of the sun's fermenting power by the serpent-like vapors of the Edenic age, and will be struck with the connection of this with the absence of fertility or procreation under that condition of things.

The processions in honor of this worship were called *phallagogia*, and the hymns sung at the time *phallikon melos*. The phallus was generally made of red leather and attached to an enormous pole. Some phalli were of great size; one carried in the procession of Ptolemy Philadelphus being one hundred and twenty yards in length, and covered with gilding. (Aristotle traces the origin of comedy to the ribald jokes made on such occasions.) Before the temple of Venus at Hieropolis stood two phalli one hundred and twenty feet high, upon which, at certain times, a priest climbed in the performance of the rites of worship.

In the mysteries of Freemasonry great use is made of the famous "point within the circle."* The writers of Masonry give the following account of the origin and meaning of this sign. In "Traditions of Masonry," p. 87, we read:—

"The mysteries among the Chinese and Japanese had similar rites. In these, a ring supported by two serpents was emblematic of the world protected by the power and wisdom of the Creator; and that is the origin of the two parallel lines (into which time has changed the two serpents) that support the circle in our lodges."

"It is evident that the sun, either as an object of worship or of symbolization, has always formed

---

* See Plate 36.

an important part of both the mysteries and the system of Freemasonry. .... The parallel lines indicate the limits of the sun's extreme northern and southern declination when he arrives at the solstitial points of Cancer and Capricorn."*

Past Grand Master Mackay, in his "Symbolism of Freemasonry," page 353, says: "The point within the circle is derived from the ancient sun worship, and is in reality of *phallic* origin. .... The lines touching the circle are said to represent St. John, the Evangelist, and St. John, the Baptist, but they really refer to the solstitial points, Cancer and Capricorn, in the Zodiac." p. 352.

"Perfectly to understand this symbol, I must refer as a preliminary matter to the worship of the phallus, a peculiar modification of sun worship, which prevailed to a great extent among the nations of antiquity. The phallus was the sculptured representation of the *membrum virile*, or male organ of generation, and the worship of it is said to have originated in Egypt, where, after the murder of Osiris by Typhon, which is symbolically

* See "Alpha and Omega," Plate 27.

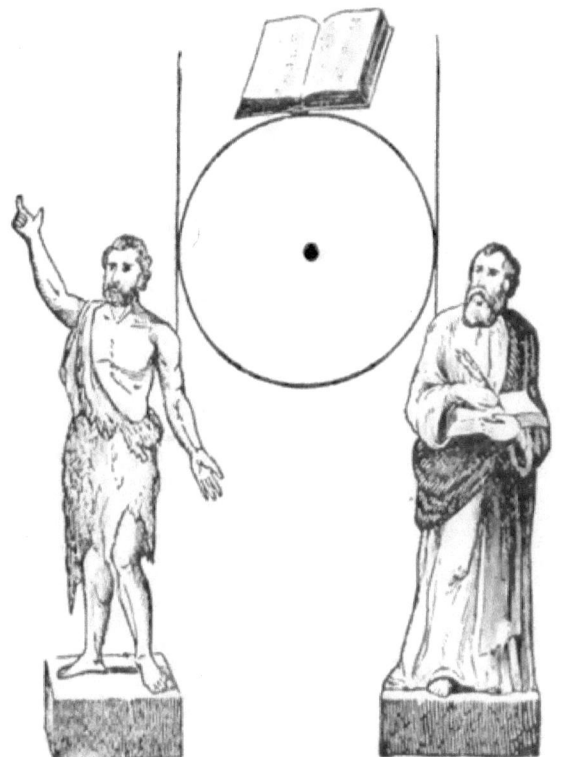

Plate 36.   THE POINT IN A CIRCLE.

THE CROSS AND PHALLIC WORSHIP. 349

to be explained as the destruction or deprivation of the sun's light by night, Isis, his wife, as the symbol of nature, in search for his mutilated body, is said to have found all the parts except the organ of generation; which myth is simply symbolic of the fact that the sun having set, its fecundating and invigorating power had ceased. The phallus, therefore, as the symbol of the male generative principle, was very universally venerated among the ancients, and that too as a religious rite." p. 112.

"Osiris is supposed by some commentators to be the god mentioned under the name of Baal-peor in the book of Numbers, as having been worshipped by the idolatrous Moabites."

In the "Manual of the Lodge" Mackay says, page 56: "The phallus was the representation of the male generative organ. It was represented usually by a column which was surrounded by a circle at its base, intended for the cteis or female generative organ. This union of the cteis and phallus, which is well represented by the point within the circle, was intended by the ancients as a type of the prolific powers of nature which they worshipped under the united forms of the active or male principle, and the passive or female principle."

In "The Lexicon of Freemasonry," page 353, we read, "The phallus was the wooden image of the *membrum virile*, which being affixed to a pole, formed a part of most of the pagan mysteries, and was worshipped as the emblem of the male generative principle. The phallic worship was first established in Egypt. From Egypt it was introduced into Greece, and its exhibition formed a part of the Dionysian mysteries. In the Indian mysteries it was called the *lingam*, and was always found in the most holy place in the temples. It was adopted by the idolatrous Israelites, who took it from the Moabites when in the Wilderness of Sin, under the name of Baal-peor."

Many people are ignorant of the fact that the cross was in existence long before the time of Christ Its origin lies in the remotest antiquity; and of that I now wish to speak. It was used as a means of punishment for a great while before the beginning of our era, but it does not appear that any connection between its use as a punishment and as a religious emblem existed until the crucifixion of Jesus.

All its forms may be resolved into four.* Of these the first was the Greek cross, composed of four equal arms, forming right angles. This is found on Assyrian tablets, Egyptian and Persian monuments, and on early Asiatic and Greek coins, as well as upon Etruscan pottery. The oblique form, or St. Andrew's cross, is also very common in ancient sculpture. The Latin cross, or *crux immissa*, occurs on monuments, medals, and coins antedating the Christian era. The *crux commissa*, called the *tau* cross from its resemblance to the Greek letter of that name, is generally considered the oldest form of the symbolic cross, and is undoubtedly the most ancient sign of the phallic mysteries and worship.† It was considered to be the symbol of the active or life-giving principle in

---

* See Plate 37.

† When the upright phallus, surrounded at the top by the circle, or cteis, is looked at from the side, the circle appears as a line crossing the upright, and the whole resembles the **T**, or tau. Hence, the cross.

nature. In this sense may be interpreted the cruciform sceptres in the hands of Astarte on Asiatic medals, and the symbols in the mysteries of Venus and of Mithra. In the *crux ansata*, the Egyptians set forth this same "sign of life," and understood it to typify the union of Isis with Osiris, or the active and passive elements. Some regard it as the symbol of eternal life, or the new life promised to neophytes after their initiation into the higher mysteries. It is very common on Egyptian monuments, and is constantly seen in the hands of Isis, Osiris, and other divinities.

This symbol was found by Layard on the sculptures of Khorsabad and on the ivory tablets of Nimrud; and it is carved on the walls of the cave temples of India. It was seen on the walls of the famous Serapeum at Alexandria, and some have supposed that it formed the basis for the well-known monogram of Christ; but this is very doubtful.

The cross was very common in the British Isles, and among the Gallic Celts. The shamrock of Ireland derives its sacredness from its resem-

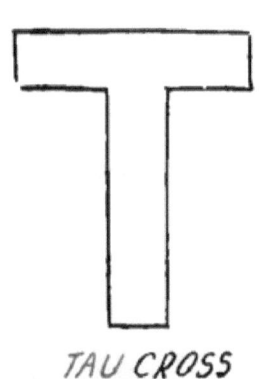

TAU CROSS
(CRUX COMMISSA)

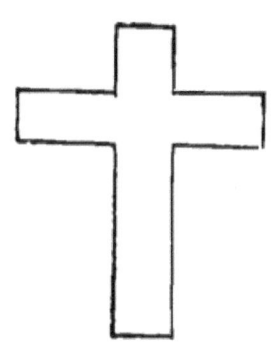

LATIN CROSS
(CRUX IMMISSA)

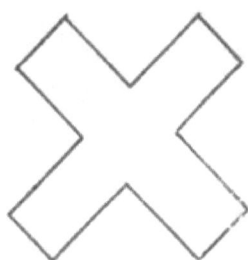

ST. ANDREWS CROSS

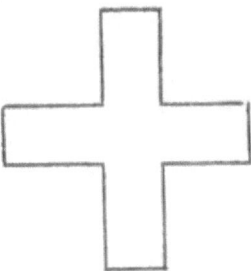

GREEK CROSS

SHAMROCK.

CRUX ANSATA

Plate 37.   VARIATIONS OF THE CROSS.

blance to it in form; and in the mysteries of the Druids the trefoil had a similar relation. In Scandinavia the hammer of the god Thor, used to bless the marriage tie, was a cross. In the shell mounds of Denmark are found cruciform hammers, probably used in sacrifices to Thor. A form of the cross is the sacred emblem of Vishnu, and of the Buddhist; it is found in Phœnician tombs, and on the oldest Greek coins, notably those of Chalcedon, Syracuse, and Corinth. The Spanish conquerors found crosses of wood erected in Mexico and in Central and South America. The Muyscas and Mayas reverenced it, and among the Toltecs it was called "the tree of nutriment" or "tree of life."

The cross was almost universally used as an instrument of torture, and of death. For this purpose all the various forms were employed. Some authorities insist that before the second century, or even later, no other form than that of the *tau* (T) exists on the tombs and monuments, and the general belief is that Christ was crucified upon a cross of that form. To this I call special attention, coupled with the undoubted fact of that being the form most particularly associated with the ancient mysteries and the phallic worship.

The church soon learned to look upon the cross as an emblem of victory rather than of disgrace, and it became the chosen symbol of Christianity. Some assert that as early as the beginning of the second century a particular efficacy began to be ascribed to it, and it was regarded with veneration (or superstition). It is found in the tombs of the catacombs as early as the second century, sometimes in company with the dove, the serpent, the fish, and other sacred emblems. But it remained for the Emperor Constantine to give it the official position upon the ensigns of his army. From that time to the present the cross has been the special sign and symbol of the Roman power, or the fourth great kingdom of the gentiles, and rules everywhere in the eastern and western divisions in one form or another. In this connection it is very noteworthy that the Reformation classed its use and worship with the abuses of Rome, and the Protestant churches have, in the main, refrained from its employment to any great extent. In this the Protestant church stands almost alone, for even the great temples of India, like those at Benares and Muttra, are cruciform in shape, while many of the Druidical structures followed the same plan in construction.

From all this, it is apparent that cross worship is but phallic worship disguised, while it is even plainer that phallic worship speaks of a time when the fecundating or seed-producing power was dormant because the solar beams were sufficiently obscured to shut out from the earth their fermenting and decaying effects.* It also seems that serpent forms were associated with the change, and that the virile principle itself came to be worshiped in connection with sun and serpent worship, while the symbols gradually passed into the form of the cross. We can see, therefore, in the latter, the concentrated symbol of original sin, and the fittest possible form on which to put to death Him who came to save from sin, and purify the fountain at the very source.

* See "Alpha and Omega."

The Phallus was worshipped as the "spring of life," or as the "tree of life." It was regarded as the source of life to all humanity. The T shaped cross or *tau* suggested the union of the two organs, and hence the reproductive function and power. In a dying earth, however, the rule and law is, "dying thou shalt die," expressing the truth that death is at work in all organisms, and decay preponderates over repair. The act of germination, or rather the condition of life which allows of seed forming and reproducing, means positively that decay is present, for decay or ferment is necessary to reproduction. So God said, " dying thou shalt die," that is, in the day, or during the period in which you eat or partake of the corruption of evil, you shall be a dying or decaying race. And it has been so.

In this connection we can see more reason in the Levitical law for the purification of women after childbirth than has been heretofore discovered. Seed forming and reproduction, being scientifically a process and transmission of ferment and corruption in excess of life and repair, placed the weight on the debit side of the balance, **and** atonement was necessary **for** the mother. She had truly and scientifically "conceived in sin."

But misguided man looked to this seed-forming power as **the real** source of life, and hence worshipped the phallus and *tau*, expressive of the union of the male and female principles. But Jesus said of the angels, and of men and women in the resurrection age, that they "neither marry nor are given in marriage." Angels do not reproduce their kind, for they know no decay whatever. We **only** reproduce that which is in danger of perishing. There is no call for a second edition till the first is about exhausted. He who continues to live in the full possession of his powers has no need for another to take his place.

Phallic worship is so ancient, but it is **at the** same time very recent. At the present day it continues in eastern countries. Only lately the government of Japan has spoken against it, and in India it still holds sway under the name of *ling* worship, the Phallus being styled *ling* or *lingam*. There is certainly a reason for the passion for reproducing oneself in the human race, a passion too widespread to call for any special comment. The Bible student knows well the strength of this ambition among the Hebrews. The story of Jephthah's daughter stands as a sample of the way in which the Jews bewailed the fate of an enforced virginity. Among heathen nations to-day we see the same instinct cropping out in the familiar wish of the Chinese, "May you become the mother of many children." Compare this with the declaration of David in Psalms cxxvii.: "Children are an heritage from the Lord. Happy is the man who has his quiver full of them."

Scientifically, therefore, in our present conditions, human life is communicated or transmitted through death. It is because we are dying that we can hand over our life to another. I challenge scientific refutation on this point. Therefore, in order to save fallen man it became necessary to reverse the cycles of sin. Life must come through death, no matter what kind of life it be. The law "after his kind" standing guard at the door of escape prevented man from ever " working out his own **salvation" by any** sort of natural process or evolution. What he needed was "eternal life," not more of the natural kind he had on hand. But in order that this eternal life could reach him in his present environment and under his present laws, it must enter his race and propagate itself by "dying."

There is the most **rigid** scientific **law here.** Christ was an "incarnation"; not a natural birth. His advent is the miracle of the ages, **and only the Great First Cause could do it.** No angel could accomplish such a miracle. Before the flood the angels took wives, but God never took a wife. His power came upon Mary, and she conceived an Immortal Son, entirely different in quality from the "sons of men." In this Immortal **Son there resided the life, "in him was life."*** But in order that this life could propagate, so to speak, in order that it could be handed over to men, it had to know **the touch of** death, even as the first Adam never generated offspring until he knew that touch Therefore Christ died for all men, for that all **have**

* John i. 4.

sinned and come short; and through that death he has opened the closed door and hands over the gift of eternal life to the race.

Here is the mighty difference between the incarnation and all the demon imitations such as the union with the women before the flood. We may grant for the sake of argument that Satan himself will be the father of the Antichrist of the last days, even as his lieutenants were the actual fathers of the antechristian race of giants in the last days of the old world; but it will be only a base imitation of the incarnation. That is the great miracle, the "mystery of Godliness," and hence is the subject of the imitations of the heathen world.

We can see, therefore, why in these last days (if they be the last) Buddhism is becoming so prominent and making converts all over Christendom. It is because it presents so strongly the doctrine of incarnations and reincarnations, tending to cheapen the miracle of the ages and pave the way for the acceptance of Antichrist as superhuman.

In Revelation ix. 20, we read that wicked men in the last days will not repent in spite of terrible judgments, and that they will continue to "worship devils." If they continue to do so, they must have been addicted to the practice before the last days. Hence we have positive Scripture for the fact that men do "worship demons" in our time as well as in the days of Moses and Joshua. A moment's thought will tell any informed person that a very large portion of mankind are devil worshippers to-day; most of Africa is given over to it, and elsewhere it is quite common. It is very easy to conclude that God never uttered such thunders against a thing which is only a figment of the fancy, and the phantasy of a dream. If the Bible be true at all it is certain that demons exist and that they can and do play a very important part in the affairs of men.

The fact that germination did not occur until after the fall of our first parents may indicate the order according to law: 1. The moral offense; 2. The altering of the environment, as explained in "Alpha and Omega," allowing ferment to actively set up its operations; and 3. The act of coition between the man and woman under the new conditions resulting in the production of offspring. In this view of the case the poison of Satan simply slumbered until the energizing effects of the new order of things produced active conception, "and sin when it was finished brought forth death." How significant that this first seed was he who first dealt actual physical death to another! Truly the law "after his kind" holds even there.

But still another suggestion may be made on the point of the slowness of germination in the beginning. As we have seen in "Alpha and Omega," the environment changed at the very time of the original sin; and changed so much as to warrant the clothing of warm skins donned by the actors in the great tragedy of life and death. Therefore ferment had begun at that very time. Now if the temptation and fall had only just occurred, of course, no offspring had yet appeared, for sufficient time had not elapsed. But now "Adam knew Eve, his wife, and she conceived and brought forth a son," etc. I suggest that many a child has been born into this world as the son of a husband, when he has been really the son of another man. (Women have often proved false to their marriage vows, and borne children which the husband supposed to be his; and it has even happened that the mother herself has been sometimes at a loss to determine precisely which man was the father of her child. Therefore, it is entirely possible that Eve, who knew nothing about the facts of obstetrics, nor of the laws of generation, may have been perfectly honest in supposing that Cain was "from the Lord," that is was the son of Adam, born in proper order and sequence, while really he was the offspring of the previous union with the demon prince.

I offer these suggestions for the benefit of the doubting mind who will not accept the declaration of the Scriptures as really meaning what it says. Certainly the Bible does most plainly declare that union with demons was and is possible, and I sincerely hope to be acquitted by all readers of originating this statement from the depths of my own fancy. I have given abundant references, and refer the reader again to them. Read them, and quarrel with the Bible if you will, but not with the author of this book, who certainly never manufactured a single one of these statements, but who believes in applying the most rigid tests of scientific law to them all, and who now submits the said application.

Why did God include in the curse the words to woman, "I will greatly multiply thy conception?" The eternal fitness of things does not fail here. Having specifically sinned by conceiving or cohabiting with the original sinner (Satan), it was fitting that the very act of sin should become the means of its transmission, and of the punishment of the transgressor. It is thinkable that cohabitation may have been possible as a sinless pleasure in Eden, at least at proper times and seasons, though of this we, of course, cannot be sure; but in the act of disobedience "sin entered, and death by sin," and, therefore, God caused offended law to bring its own requital, and to be measured unto her again with heaping measure—"greatly multiplied."

Some may ask why, if this strange union with demons produced offspring before the flood, does it not do so now, provided it is really practiced? In replying to this we must remember all the terrible declarations of the Old Testament concerning the specific sin of the Canaanites and of some of the people of Israel. Beyond all possible dispute, we are overwhelmingly assured that those people did actually become " mistresses of demons," and that even men had "a familiar spirit." And it is equally sure that the most terrific thunders of judgment were pronounced against those who in any way entered into such a state.

It is a little difficult to see why God should speak so very severely and assign such fearful punishments if all that was done was simply to talk with spirits, that is, to only become a medium in the sense of communicating thoughts to and receiving them from beings of another sphere. But the great fact stands out before us that God exhausted language in denouncing the sin, and absolutely exterminated all who touched it in any way.

However lightly some reader may see fit to regard this sin, the Allwise God seemed to look upon it as *the plague of the universe,* and to esteem nothing too severe as a disinfectant or preventive.

(If, however, the language of Scripture be taken in its plain and ordinary sense, and we really accept its declarations that women, and perhaps men, entered into such relations with wicked spirits as to positively know something at least similar to sexual intercourse, thereby receiving into their mortal flesh the very spawn of hell, and becoming tainted through and through with the essence of evil, the action and words of the Almighty begin to appear somewhat more reasonable, and the punishments assigned take upon them the nature of necessary scientific fumigation and purification for the actual life and safety of the rest of the race, not to speak of the demands of grieved and offended justice.)

Reading the record with care, we are impressed that the extraordinary race of giants found in and near Canaan were closely akin to those who appeared upon the scene just before the flood. The parentage of the latter we certainly know, for the Word declares it; they were the sons of the wicked angels by the daughters of the antediluvian race. In the case of the Canaanitish giants, we are not told so positively that they were of demon descent, but as union with the demons was most specifically the great sin of their people, and as they were specially doomed to extermination by the word of the Lord, and the reason of this special sin assigned for their destruction, the conclusion seems very well sustained that they also were of the evil strain. A close study of the Hebrew words used to designate these giants, gives much strength to the above argument. Hence, I conclude that there is almost nothing against the belief that the Anakim and others of like structure were partly, at least, the offspring of the unnatural union with spirits for which they and their parents were sentenced to absolute extermination.

Some one will now ask why such giants are not now seen on the earth? and whether there is any evidence that offspring now exist as a result of this demon intercourse. By way of preliminary answer I call attention again to the express declarations that in the last times men shall "worship devils," and that a widespread attention shall be given to "seducing spirits, who forbid to marry," etc., and to all other texts we have considered in connection with these—the necessity for women in this age to have their heads covered "because of the angels," the tendency to be led captive as "silly women" by seducers, etc., etc. Surely there is much in the Bible to warrant the understanding of the word of Christ, that "as it was in the days of Noah so shall it be in the days of the son of man," which we have already given; that is, that the very sins of Noah's day shall be reproduced. And beyond dispute this was the great and crowning sin of his time.

A suggestion along the lines of truth discussed in "Alpha and Omega" may be pertinent here. Evolutionists are very ready to claim that "missing links" might be found if only the environment and conditions were more favorable to such developments than at present. I accept this suggestion far enough to say that it is thinkable that the en-

Plate 38. THE BREADTH OF REDEMPTION

vironment of the antediluvian age was more favorable to the actual development of the demon seed than in any age since that time. Surely this is scientific, the evolutionist being witness. As we see in "Alpha and Omega," the lingering vapors in the sky after the flood certainly did affect the span of life until the days of Moses and Joshua, and it may be that under such conditions the development of the evil progeny was more possible than at the present day.

But if we are approaching the crisis, and the Coming Age is looming above the horizon, it is entirely possible that some magnetic quality in the environment may reach us in advance of the crash; some effect as sudden and mysterious as la grippe may sweep down among us, and touch the life principle in the race in such a way that the old result may again appear, and offspring like those of the days of Noah once more curse the earth. Certainly we do now see giants in wickedness as perhaps never before. And it is noticeable that the wickedness of our day takes the form and garb of the intellectual rather than the brutal.

Even in the mighty preparations now being made on every hand for the last great and awful war which all agree will convulse this planet as none other ever did, this intellectual, and if you please, this refined disguise, is universally adopted. But the seeker after truth looks deeper than the surface, and sees in the frightful engines of war, the terrible high explosives, the general mobilization of the armies, the gigantic loans and debts all on account of war, while professedly "to preserve the peace," and in the growing indifference to the death and destruction of multitudes instead of individuals,— the truth seeker, I say, sees in all these infallible signs that wickedness has its "giant offspring" in one very important sense at least. And he who remembers that the whole is simply of a kind with its parts must conclude that there are individual giants of evil under and back of all this national strife and sin.

I cannot tell just what elements are necessary in the environment to allow of the reappearance upon the earth of the physical giants of previous ages, but I surely know that a scientific reason must have obtained for their existence at all What scientist will dare to dispute the assertion that when a whole race was of gigantic stature, or when a large number of such giants abounded, there must have been a reason in the surroundings and conditions of life to account for it. And who will deny the possibility of the incoming of some influence upon the earth which may revive or reproduce such growths? Those who read the chapter on "The War of the Stars" in "Alpha and Omega" will see facts that cause the most solemn thoughts in many great minds. The conjunction of the giant planets may possibly send us such an influence as that of which I have just spoken. I merely suggest; assertion would be very foolish; but as such conditions did once exist, and as I know there must have been a natural reason then, so, if such things are to be again, the same or equally operative causes must come in.

Scripture does not plainly say that Antichrist will be the actual son of Satan by a human mother; but in the light of all that it does say, and the many facts herein presented, there certainly seems to be a very strong probability for that conclusion. And if this unnatural union between spirits and our race once produced offspring, there is certainly no scientific reason why it may not do so again. To dogmatise to the contrary, in the presence of all the facts studied in this book, is certainly very unwise.

(In the light of all this it will be better seen how much fallen man really is, when we find him in all ages worshipping the very thing which, in its abuse (note carefully, not in its proper use, but its abuse), brought in sin and death. The *phallus* and *cteis* have been enthroned as deities, and the unclean *tau*, or cross, made the symbol of religion in all countries. But it also shows the marvelous depths of salvation which stoops to man just where he is, and hesitates not to touch and transform the very emblem of sin itself and cover it with the shining glories of Heaven and of God. Man is the victim of sin; he is "conceived in sin" without his own consent; born into a world of sin whether he will or no, and finds himself overwhelmed by its terrible effects working death in him in spite of all he can do. Therefore it is just that a " way of escape " be offered him, and fitting that this way is such as to exactly reverse all the conditions of the fall, and tracing the steps backward, actually bring life out of death

CHAPTER VI.

The Mystery of Iniquity.

FROM the heights of Eden, let us review the marshaled ranks of facts and theory which we have gathered.

It is prehistoric time. Man has not yet appeared on the planet; but over its wonderful surface, in the midst of the stones of fire, moves the covering cherub, he who "sealed up the sum, perfect in beauty," Lucifer, the son of the morning, the prince of this world, and the chief of the archangels of God. By some strange inworking of thought, his "heart becomes lifted up because of his beauty," and "iniquity was found in him," and God cast him down.*

---

* For a full discussion of the nature of Satan and of angels in general, see "Alpha and Omega," chapter on "Satan."

Chaos ensues, and the world whirls through **space,** a darkened sphere, "without form and void." But "God said, let there be light," and forth from **the chaos came** cosmos in all its order and beauty. "And God saw that it was very **good."** But **a new lord and** ruler must be found, and after all else had been done, God formed man **in** his own image, and gave to him the **new** world **as his domain.** At once Lucifer rages with **jealousy and hate.** This being, to whom all the new creation bow in unquestioning submission, must **be** destroyed by some means, and God's plan thwarted, whatever it may be. Carefully the campaign is planned. **The weakest** point in the defenses **is** eagerly sought; and by comparison with the **brute** creation, the sex principle is shrewdly selected as the most powerful and **far-**reaching in its influences and consequences.

The time is chosen carefully when the rising tide in the blood first begins **to** make itself felt, but before it has reached its highest mark and its **full** significance discovered. Eve is approached **with** temptation disguised "as an angel of light," promising greater revelations of truth, and yet casting a doubt on the simple word of the Lord. Utterly innocent and entirely ignorant of sin, she yields the point of vantage to the "higher criticism" of the wise archangel, and, looking on the temptation in the light of his suggestion, sees it suddenly become "a thing to be desired and to make one wise." Undue and unnatural excitation is applied to the organism, and the woman becomes "the mistress of a demon," thinking him to be an angel of light. A little later, and the evil knowledge of the unnatural possibilities is communicated to the man; he yields to the temptation exerted upon him by the excited state of the woman, and gives up his will also to the temptation — and

PARADISE IS LOST!

God comes down to see what has been done, and the searching question, "Where art thou?" brings the guilty pair before him. The curse is pronounced, first upon the serpent, and the promise of a Mighty Deliverer to come through the very seed, which the tempter thought hopelessly poisoned for all time, is given. The announcement of the changed condition of the woman, and of her subjection to her husband's will and desire, follows; and then the clothing of skins recognizes the new-found shame, and, at the same time, the blood of sacrifice for sin. The climate changes, cold comes in, decay begins, and the Edenic state has gone into the past.

Cain is born, but Satan guesses he is not the promised seed, and begins at once his evil working. The smoke of Abel's sacrifice has hardly cleared away when the blood of the first martyr reddens the earth, and the long, long tragedy of the race begins. Courage, archangel! you may yet defeat the divine plans. With renewed energy the adversary bends to his work, and down through the centuries only a mere scarlet line stretches across the dark, dark page of antediluvian history. "And God saw that the wickedness of man was great in the earth, and that every imagination of the thoughts of his heart was evil, and only evil continually." The whole world was filled with iniquity.

But the dragging centuries, with their poisoned fruit, are too slow for the seething hate of the serpent, and some quicker means for the destruction of the detested race must be found. In a moment of hellish inspiration, the lieutenants of the Satanic host decide to imitate the example of their captain, and completely pollute the blood of the entire generation. The plan is approved, and the " demons (originally sons, or creatures of God), saw the daughters of men that they were fair, and took them wives of all whom they chose."

This time there was no disguise. "Higher criticism" had borne its legitimate fruit. Nobody had to be "deceived" now; for all were sunken in iniquity. The demon lovers " came in unto the daughters of men, and they bare children to them, the same becoming men of renown" — renown in wickedness, naturally inherited from their parents. The deed was done; the end was accomplished; the whole race was poisoned hopelessly beyond redemption; the iniquity of the generation was full; and there could be no possible remedy, and no safety for the single, lonely line of the children of Seth, but the absolute destruction of the entire race.

Noah's preaching fell upon careless ears, as Enoch's had done before him. Eating and drinking, marrying and giving in marriage — the gratification of all the fleshly appetites to the full, aided by the sciences and inventions of fifteen hundred years, and intensified by the evil power of the blood of the demigods — these were the occupations of the fallen multitudes, until the day that Noah entered into the ark, and God shut him in.

Terror strikes through the ranks of hell as the swirling waters of the mighty catyclysm engulf their giant progeny, and fallen mothers, in one common and terrible destruction. Has the Almighty determined on their destruction also? And over the howling of the tempest arise the shrieks of fear from the demon hosts, and of hatred of the God of a judgment so long delayed.

But courage, archangel! these who emerge from the ark, are the same kind of men. To the attack! They are no stronger than their fathers. And surely the result justifies the belief, for under the shade of Noah's sacrifice the old secret of shame is touched again, and the curse falls upon Canaan, from whose loins are to proceed the seven nations, upon whom descends the same fearful sin that will finally bring their "iniquity to the full."

The powers of evil take heart once more and soon, upon the plains of Babel, God is set at naught by the unbelieving crew, who strive to build a monument so high that no deluge can ever reach its summit. Again the hand of the Almighty is stretched forth in judgment, and the tribes disperse to the four winds, as confusion falls upon the tongue, and fear fills the heart. But Satan rallies his cohorts, and speedily spreads the seeds of idolatry among the fallen race. The sun, which apparently had driven away the vapor roof of the previous age,* and whose terrible power for heat and climatic changes is now felt for the first time, must be propitiated; while the arching serpents in the northern heavens gradually disappearing in polar snows furnish foundation for myth and marvel, and thus begins the long line of

.* See "Alpha and Omega."

superstitions and idolatrous practices, whose very names are legion, and whose rites and orgies have deluged the world with blood and shame.

Another effort of divine love and mercy calls out Abraham, that the experiment of a select and isolated people may be tried. But what cares Lucifer? Promises of future "seed" are not feared. He lives and works in the great present, and wages war against his Creator while he can. Only a few years, and the chosen race languish in Egyptian bondage, and with desperate purpose the powers of this world are inspired to destroy the line through which the Lord had said the promised "seed" should come. And so successful is the effort that once more the Almighty has to stretch forth his hand in consuming judgments, that through the crystal gates of the divided sea, the marching hosts of Israel may reach the shore of freedom for which they had prayed.

Is Lucifer discouraged? No, not yet. Pausing not to mourn his allies, drowned in the avenging waters, he stirs the hearts of the newly emancipated slaves to rebellion, and the people murmur at

Marah, and wish for the flesh of Egypt. A little later Mount Sinai is "altogether on a smoke," and from the thick darkness comes the voice that shakes the earth and the sea, and to which no created flesh can listen unmoved. But the daring demon dashes among the hosts, and even while Moses and Jehovah commune together on the mountain's summit, at its base the jewels are flung in the furnace, and around the golden calf the people join hands in sin once more.*

Surely God will give up the fight, and wipe out the offending race. Ah, listen! That is very nearly what He proposes to his faithful servant; but Moses' prayers prevail, and the desert march is begun. Again the battle is pressed, and soon the people cry for flesh; and, while the recollection of the fate of those who ate is still fresh in their minds, the same old sin is brought in again, and the Midianitish woman is taken to the tent of the

---

* The phallic emblems were placed upon the temple of the god Apis — the sacred bull. The ten plagues that fell upon Egypt had each a distinct reference to, and fitness for, a special god, and a special branch of the Egyptian idolatry, just as in the case of the Philistines, already noticed on page 266.

man of Simeon. Judgment again falls, sharp and terrible, for God will not sit still very long when that old trump card of the Devil is played; but the sin goes on, and heathen wives henceforth form the chief allies of the great adversary.

Joshua leads the nation into Canaan, but his body is hardly cold in death before the worship of Astarte in all its filthy and cruel horrors sweeps in, and captivity follows captivity for four hundred years. The demon-filled women of Canaan are too much for Israel. (Even Samson, the strongest of men, lays his head down in Delilah's lap, and dies with his enemies in the temple of Dagon.* The wives multiply; the groves rise everywhere; the children pass through the fire unto Molech; diviners abound; the living seek unto the dead (literally "to the spirits of Python") and wizards arise on every hand, while the "woman, the mistress of a demon" is ready with her infernal arts to lead other souls into the captivity of hell. (Will the daughters of Eve never cease to follow their mother's footsteps! And the

* The god of the phallic worship.

sons of Adam not learn to refuse to join with them? No, not in this age.)

The kings are allowed to take the rule, and the "man after God's own heart" begins so well that Satan's work is checked. But even he falls with a Hittite woman,* and his splendid son builds a palace for Pharoah's daughter, and adds hundreds of the forbidden races to his harem. It is not long before Ahab seeks out the daughter of the Astarte-worshipping Zidonians, and the name of Jezebel is stamped upon the history and "mystery of iniquity" in letters of unfading fire, while Manasseh adopts all the sins of the Canaanitish people; and soon the tribes go into captivity once more, in which state the nameless abominations multiply of which we have only the hints of Ezekiel, but are spared the awful details.† Courage! Again,

---

* Who thus became one of the direct ancestors of Christ, making it possible for the Incarnation to scientifically touch the very bottom of the pit of sin, that the lowest might be saved.

† See Ezekiel viii. 7-16. The "weeping for Tammuz" spoken of by Ezekiel, was a rite in the worship of the sun, and closely connected with the unclean "mysteries of Baal-peor," as the **T** or *tau* with which Tammuz begins signified. Writers on Freemasonry identify Tammuz with Adonis, upon whom the sensual goddess Venus lavished her desires.

Archangel, you may yet succeed in defeating Jehovah. Certainly the laboring centuries have so far produced nothing but sin, and its results; but a wonderful change is at hand.

Yet once more God puts forth his hand; and this time the primal promise is suddenly brought upon the scene. The power of the highest overshadows the simple Jewish maiden. How Satan had laughed at the possibility of its fulfillment. Had he not poisoned the entire blood of the race?* And was not the law "after his kind" absolutely opposed to the "seed of the woman" ever being anything but sinful? It could not be. But "with God all things are possible," and even this was not excepted. "A body thou hast prepared me."† Ah! Lucifer forgot that the God who arbitrarily creates, can as arbitrarily purge if He see fit. The absolute consecration of the lowly Mary, "Be it unto me even as thou wilt," enthrones the will of the Lord, and at that will takes place the Incarnation—a conception without the taint of sin. As

---

* Even the line of Christ, through the Hittite, Bathsheba.
† Hebrews x. 5.

always, the son is counted from the father, and thus appeared another spotless creation, the second Adam, made in the likeness of God, and the express image of His person, the only pure birth that ever took place among the race of man. "That holy thing that shall be born of thee!"* How many rise up just now to dispute that assertion of the angel! In the ranks of the most spiritual multiply those who fall under the old heresy of a "carnal nature in Christ, inherited from His mother."† Truly the very spirit of the age is only Antichrist.

The wonderful scene by Jordan's banks follows, where the great archangel strove in vain for the mastery. The second Adam "kept his garments"‡ spotless, and the specious plea for a moment's "worship" was hurled back from the sinless heart of the Son of Man. Authority was asserted, and at the "Get thee hence, Satan!" the first manifest bruising of the serpent's head

---

* Luke i. 35.

† Why the agitation of that particular heresy just at this time? Surely all lines converge to the great focus of the age.

‡ Revelation xvi. 15.

began. But with courage that would be splendid in a good cause, the fallen spirit returned to the fight, through his human allies. Rejection followed rejection, and from the gates which had opened to receive the humble King upon the ass's colt the dishonered Lord walked forth to return no more, and the doom was pronounced upon the rebellious nation.

With redoubled energy the battle is pressed; the traitor is found even among the "chosen" twelve; Gethsemane, the scourging, the crown of thorns, the judgment hall, the death sentence, the weary, struggling march beneath the heavy cross, the taunts of the multitude — Calvary! How fast the crowding eagles * troop to the Demon's standard! What a wonderful day in the history of sin!

The cross! Ah! few of us know its dark and dreadful meaning. We think of it as a type, but are ignorant of its hellish significance. But that I feel that these are truly the last days, and that the truth in all its fearful power is needed for the

* Luke xvii. 37.

conflict with the Man of Sin, I would never have written the truth on this point. So many memories cluster round the cross on which the Redeemer of men gave up his life. So many millions of lips have been pressed to the symbol of the cross in devout recognition of Him whose blood was shed for our sins. So many voices have joined in the mighty anthem of those who, with Paul, glory in naught "save in the cross of Jesus Christ." Yet I believe that the truth, rightly understood, will only serve to intensify these feelings of reverence and awe, as we stand before the cross.

The cross was not good in itself. As well try to make a friend of death. The cross was accurst as was every one who died thereon. Hence Jesus "was made a curse for us, for it is written, Cursed is every one that hangeth on a tree."* It is only the power and presence of Him who hung upon it that makes the cross of any importance to us. Therefore, when I say that the cross was from all antiquity the most concentrated emblem and sign of the foulest filth and sin, and reveal the fact that

* Galatians iii. 13.

it was the famous phallic emblem, called by the unclean devotees of the vile mysteries, the "sign of life," I do not in any sense touch a sacred thing, for the cross was never that. He who was holy and sacred hung upon it, but it was only vile. But now mark the double significance.

About that fated spot the hosts of hell sweep round with intensest hate and fiendish delight, as the wonderful being of whom the voice had spoken the tremendous words, "This is my beloved Son," rejected by those he came to save, deserted by his friends, and left without manifestation of miraculous power by the Almighty, is finally nailed to the vile and cursed cross. Surely Archangel! thy triumph has come at last. Victorious in Eden, but trembling at the promise of the wondrous seed of the woman, the great leader of the demon hosts has waged successful war all along the centuries, with but occasional defeats, until in the Jordan wilderness the second Adam hurls him back without the slightest acceptance of the temptation. But now the end is accomplished in another way. To the first Adam the word was given, "Thou shalt surely die," but to the second death is brought and forced upon him. If he die, victory rests upon the banners of hell; and if he die polluted by the curse of the foul heathen symbol, and thus becomes a curse, how can he ever redeem others when himself he has become unclean?

Calvary is reached; the motley procession halts; the unresisting form is stretched upon the fearful symbol; with resounding blows the cruel nails are driven through the tender flesh; the instrument of torture and of death is erected, and set in the rock; and before the universe He, who himself was the Life of men, dies upon the intensive emblem of the very deepest abyss of sin into which their evil hearts and hellish tempters had plunged the race. How the demons howled in hoarse acclaim the chorus of their exultation over the fall of the second federal head of the hated race!*

* The ancient traditions held that the tree of knowledge stood upon Calvary, and near by the tree of life. If the site of our first parent's residence was at Jerusalem, the types and analogies are very full. There *the sin* was committed by which came death to all, and there the Second

But see! Terror strikes again through the unclean ranks as the dying head is lifted and the shout of triumph "It is finished!" rings through the depths of the most distant space. The darkness falls, the dead come forth! What can this mean? Their cursed "sign of life" cannot account for the bursting tombs and rending veil. The hours pass quickly, and as the third day is breaking, with sudden sweep of regal power the depths of hell itself are invaded by a single warrior. With kingly stride he moves through the dread abode of death, and without touch or word, but merely at the motion of his supreme will, binds the awful king in chains that can never part, and with the greatest monarch at his chariot wheels that ever graced the triumph of a conqueror, the Lord of Life and Glory "led captivity captive," while the escorting "twelve legions of angels" for which he could have called even at Pilate's judg-

---

Adam by his death brought life for all. There Cain was born, the seal and evidence of the birth of sin; and there was given by the blood the seal and power of the "new birth," whereby "Christ is formed within us, the hope of glory." From the hill adjacent, where grew the olives — the type of life — **He ascended;** and there He will descend bringing life eternal to his people.

ment seat, and for whom he now "presently" asked his Father,* in heavenly harmonies chanted the anthem of welcome, "Lift up your heads, Oh! ye gates, and be ye lifted up ye everlasting doors, and the King of Glory shall come in!"† And as they marched and sang, from the battlements of the Eternal City swept down the question. "Who is the King of Glory?" Hark to the answer, ye demon hosts, watching the triumphal progress of your Conqueror from the depths of the pit; listen, and know. With the full strength of the twelve legions of holy voices swells up the mighty answer,—

"The Lord of Hosts, He is the King of Glory!"

The miracle of the ages is accomplished. Out of the very jaws of death has been wrested life. The Saviour of men has not hesitated to stoop to the very bottom of all the iniquity of the crowding centuries, so that no soul of man can ever rise and say, He did not meet my case. Into the depths of our sin our Lord has plunged, yes, even to the unclean phallic sign and all that it implied, has he

* Matthew xxvi. 53.   † Psalms xxiv.

Plate 40.   THE HEIGHT OF REDEMPTION

carried his mighty salvation. The primal promise is fulfilled; "the seed of the woman has bruised the serpent's head," and the doors of a free and full redemption stand open to the fallen race. The wrath of man and of devils is "made to praise him,"* and even the vile and terrible cross is so hidden by the precious blood of Him who hung upon it that its very nature is changed, and with united voices we sing:—

> "In the cross of Christ I glory,
> Towering o'er the wrecks of time;
> All the wealth of sacred story
> Hovers round its head sublime."

The blood cleanseth even the vilest, and the resurrection life and light glorify that which was "dead in trespasses and sin." "How unsearchable are thy judgments, O God! And thy ways past finding out!"

* Psalms lxxvi. 10.

CHAPTER VII.

The Climax.

BUT the end is not yet. The mystery of iniquity still works, though with the certainty of final defeat. Pentecost again strikes terror into the demon ranks, but always eager to disbelieve God, the opportunity is seized to again try the power of temptation upon men. This new church is made of the same kind of people; they have succeeded every time before in causing them to fall. To the attack once more!

The names of the thousands are scarcely enrolled when "Satan fills the heart of Ananias and his wife to lie to the Holy Ghost."* Judgment falls, but the battle presses on. A few days later

* Acts v. 3.

the widows cause the first schism in the infant church,* and the long line of difficulties and devices begins, which have ever since occupied the hands and minds of the mass of the members much more than the work of saving souls. Politics in the church! Adopt the ways of the world! These be thy weapons, Archangel! for the new dispensation. Courage once again! The "leavening"† goes on rapidly, so rapidly that in the first two centuries the special heresies originating in the Christian church number some two thousand. One of these sects taught that Cain was the holy seed, and the sons of Seth the evil, and called themselves "Cainites"; while another, going still further, styled themselves the "Ophites," or serpent worshippers, and deified the serpent of Eden himself. Truly, it does not take long to defeat the followers of the Nazarene, however invincible he himself had proved to be.

But the old weapon is too effective to be allowed to rust. The mysteries must be revived. Ah! they had never died. From Egypt these

---

* Acts vi. 1. † Matthew xiii. 33.

mysteries had moved to Babylon, where they flourished in the days of the Chaldeans and magicians of that wonderful empire. With the decline of Babylon, after the conquest of Alexander, the teachers and priests of these abominations found their way to Pergamos, where they were in power and authority in the time of Christ. Remembering this, we are able to fully understand the double statement of the Lord to John in Revelation ii. 13, "Where Satan's seat is," and "Where Satan dwelleth." Reading on, we see that at Pergamos were those who held, "the doctrine of Balaam, who taught Balak to cast a stumbling block before the children of Israel, to eat things sacrificed unto idols, and to commit fornication."

We must pause here a moment to show the force of this reference to Balaam and Balak. Notice that both Peter and Jude, in the terrible utterances we have already discussed, mention this matter of Balaam. And here is the Lord himself, speaking to John, at the very end of the sacred canon, alluding in a special manner to the identical thing. In the message to the church at Thy-

THE CLIMAX.

atira, in the next verses, the same charge is brought, and Jesus says that this particular sin is "The depths of Satan."*

Turning back to Numbers xxiv. and xxv. we find that, immediately following the prophecy of Balaam, "Israel began to commit whoredom with the daughters of Moab. And Israel joined himself to Baal-peor; and the anger of the Lord was kindled against Israel. And Moses said unto the judges of Israel, Slay ye every one his men that were joined to Baal-peor." But just as this sentence had gone forth the man of Simeon, Zimri by name, took the Midianitish princess, Cozbi, to his tent "in the sight of all Israel." And then it was that "Phineas, the son of Aaron, rose up from among the congregation, and took a javelin in his hand; and he went after the man of Israel into the tent, and thrust both of them through, the man of Israel, and the woman through her belly. So the plague was stayed from the children of Israel." For this God specially commended Phineas, and gave to him and his seed the "cove-

* Revelation ii. 24.

nant of peace," and to this Malachi alludes a thousand years later. Moses specially refers to this great sin in Deuteronomy iv. 3, where he mentions the fact that all the men who participated in it had been destroyed. Paul refers to it in I. Corinthians x. 8, and David in Psalms cvi. 29, mentions it as coupled with the " sacrifices of the dead," thus bringing to mind the depths of Spiritualism. Certainly the sin was very great to secure so frequent mention in the Scripture.

From this brief analysis, it is clear that the very same sins upon which God had sent such terrific judgments in the wilderness, and which had been distinctly described as, " offering sacrifice to devils [demons] after whom they had gone a whoring" (Leviticus xvii. 7), and as having familiar spirits, etc., were now to be found at Pergamos and at Thyatira. And these sins are expressly identified with those taught by Balaam through Balak, which, as we have seen, both Peter and Jude distinctly describe as being the sin of sexual intercourse with demons, for which the angels that sinned are reserved unto fire, and

Sodom and Gomorrah suffered the vengeance of eternal fire. How wonderfully the unaided word of the Lord by its cross references makes clear the whole thing to one who runs!

The church at Pergamos, then, as well as at Thyatira, is warned to repent and to hold fast, while those among them who had this doctrine are included in the doom pronounced against all such sinners. And all this before the Apostles themselves had gone to join their risen Lord. Truly, Satan's leaven worked quickly.

A little later, and the mysteries had moved again, this time much farther west; and on the banks of the Tiber they found a home and resting place. Here the same abominations were taught under slightly different names; but the mysteries were the old, old iniquities that have marked the footsteps of Lucifer through the ages. Meanwhile the leaven of worldly methods and means had been working in the church. The search for power to supply the place of the lost Holy Ghost of Pentecost resulted in the great compromise act, when Constantine went through the farce of a simulated conversion, and the council of Nice legislated the marriage of the church and the world — a marriage that has known no divorce in all the centuries since, and will not know any until the Lord himself appears in flaming fire to burn up all such bonds of Satan's forging.

The heathen soldiers were ordered to carry on their sun worship on the first day of the week, and the day was called "Sunday." Previously the Christians and heathen worshipped on different days, but this adroit stratagem of the wily emperor blotted out the evident distinction, while the name of the day satisfied the heathen for the change of the time for their worship. Then the great phallic emblem, the obscene "sign of life," was foisted upon the Christians, as the emblem of their religion (it had not been so used up to this time), and the thing was arranged well enough to suit the devil himself, for, from that day to this, the world has disported in the plumes of the church, and the church has borrowed the garb of the world, until the difference between a churchly world and a worldly church passes the power of any human microscope to discern.

In the west the names were changed to suit the advance in thought, and in deference to the Christians. The "Queen of heaven" became "The Mother of God"; the "forbidding to marry, and commanding to abstain from meats," which marked the religions of the eastern mystics, were bodily transplanted into the new soil; and the angel, looking at the rapid transformation, and considering the long centuries of uncleanness to come, styled Rome, "*Mystery Babylon the Great; the mother of harlots and abominations of the earth.*" Revelation xvii. 5.

Surely the great adversary prospers wonderfully in his warfare. (We read of the Pope Alexander, father and lover of the vile Lucretia; of the general adulteries of the priests, as recorded by their own historians; and of the unspeakable vileness of monks and nuns, much of which is too horribly filthy to be recorded at all, except in Latin notes that no one has the temerity to translate.) Even the saintly Pio Nono issues the order providing for the "Priest's Retreat," where the comeliest nuns shall be kept for the use of the "holy fathers," while the unspeakable horrors of the confessional have filled even the writings of Catholic historians with protests and wishes for a purging of the old leaven. But it works steadily on.

But even all this is too slow for Lucifer. In great wrath, knowing that his time is short, his minions busily seek to revive the old mysteries in all their power and significance. Again, woman is urged to stretch forth her hand for knowledge; and, as with uncovered head, forgetting the angels,* she reaches after the promised good, on every hand she is solicited towards spirit loves and alliances. Dressed as "angels of light,"† the demons come. From Europe and Asia, from the fastnesses of Thibet, and the temples of India, from the philosophies of infidel states, and from the islands of the sea, the cry is, "mysteries!" Ah! we have it. "Esoteric;" that is the word. It means "hidden," and stands in direct antago-

---

* I. Corinthians xi. 10. † II. Corinthians xi. 14.

nism to the simplicity of the living Gospel, which is always "exoteric"—outward, on the surface. But the cry is very taking with the herd of knowledge seekers.

The beautiful in art is worshipped; nature is perverted; the flesh is considered coarse; the new philosophy turns to the realm of mind. There is no such thing as matter; it is only an idea. Now the light breaks — spirit is the only reality. Hence we must abstract ourselves entirely from the seen, and revel in the unseen; and, as we do so, we find all the desires filled and more than gratified with spirit. The angel of light must have an orthodox name to deceive the very elect. How will Christian Science answer? Most admirably, for the age is scientific, and the elect must be caught with a bait that seems to be Christian. So the old, old game is played once more; the same old trump card that won Eden is thrown down on the table of this age, with the confidence born of countless successes, and the end draws on apace.

But the ancient desire in the breast of the great Archangel urges him on to a final effort. Worship must be secured at any cost. Not permitted to appear in actual presence himself, he determines to make one supreme attempt. The greatest of the manifestations and works of the Almighty shall be imitated. The Son of God shall be counterfeited, and Satan himself makes the last attack upon our unfortunate race, just as he began it. With the first woman the fall was accomplished. With a woman of the last generation Lucifer imitates the miracle of Bethlehem's manger, and the mimic incarnation of the fallen archangel appears, born of a human mother. The ravings of the Theosophists about a second Eve are only too well founded; but instead of saving the race, as they teach, she will bring forth the "Man of Sin," the personal Antichrist of the last times.

To him the dragon gives his, "power, seat, and authority";* and to him the recreant sons of men bring their adulation, their praise, and their worship. Like his great type—Nebuchadnezzar,—he makes an image, and decrees the death of those who will not worship it, but his image is his

* Revelation xiii. 2.

own likeness. He shall sum up all power in himself; no man shall buy or sell without his mark. "fiat money" will take the markets of the world, instead of the "gold of the kingdom." His word shall be the law, and "**all** the world wonders after him." The apotheosis of evil has come at last, and Satan is triumphant. Religions are swept away. "Science **falsely so called**"* is exalted, for he "shall worship **the god of forces**."† Creeds must be given up. And through all runs the tale of the fornications which the **kings of the earth** and the nations **have drunk with her**, the **great capital of the last and universal kingdom of evil**.

In the mighty city, Babylon, the wealth of the nations concentrates, and the traffic is in, "The merchandise of gold and silver, and precious stones, and of pearls, and fine linen, and purple, and silk, and scarlet, and all thyine wood, **and** all manner vessels of ivory, and all manner vessels of most precious wood, and of brass, and iron, and marble,

---

* I. Timothy vi. 20.
† Daniel xi. 38. See in this connection the chapter on "Satan," in "Alpha and Omega" for the relationship between angels and forces.

and cinnamon, and odors, and ointments, and frankincense, and wine, and oil, and fine flour, and wheat, and beasts, and sheep, and horses, and chariots, and slaves [or bodies], and souls of men."* No wonder the angel cries, "mightily with a strong voice, saying, Babylon the great is fallen, and is become the habitation of demons, and the hold of every foul spirit, and a cage of every unclean and hateful bird. For all nations have drunk of the wine of her fornication, and the kings of the earth have committed fornication with her. . . . . Come out of her, my people, that ye be not partakers of her sins, and that ye receive not of her plagues. For her sins have reached unto heaven, and God hath remembered her iniquities."†

But the darkest hour is just before the morning. Looking backward through the mist of the sinful centuries, the figure of Cain, who "was of that wicked one," stands next to Paradise Lost. Looking forward through the rapidly breaking clouds which hide the coming day, the Man of Sin, who is

* Revelation xviii. 12, 13. † Revelation xviii. 2-4.

the concentrated incarnation of that same wicked one, stands next to **Paradise Regained**. God must needs reverse the whole sad history, and that reversal leads to the gate of Eden restored over all the sin and shame of the first days of the fall of man. The end is at the beginning. The numerator and the denominator are the same. The equation is struck. The age rounds up without a remainder. The iniquity comes to the full.

But hark! A sound is breaking upon the ears of a startled universe. Let it ring, and ring again:—

BEHOLD! THE BRIDEGROOM COMETH!

With **thunderous, whirling wheels, and lurid lightning's flash, amid the throes of a quaking, dying earth; behold** Him coming! Not a woman, but the seed of the woman; not the coming **man, but the Son of Man; not in** degradation and hu**mility, but in** exaltation and power; not with **visage marred more** than the sons of men,[*] but with countenance like unto the sun shining in his **strength;** not like a, "sheep dumb before her

---

[*] Isaiah lii. 14.

shearers,"* but with a, "voice like the sound of many waters"; not deserted by his disciples, but with thousand thousands of angelic followers the King comes for his own.

He "was manifested to destroy the works of the devil,"† (but now He comes to destroy the devil himself, and the death that has so long been in the devil's power. The waters of the deluge regenerated the earth, sweeping away the old sins, and casting them in the depths of the sea; but the flood of fire comes to sanctify the world, and burn up the roots of all evil. The "great chain"‡ is almost forged; the mighty angel is ready to descend. In another hour, or day, or year, the waiting saints will have been "caught up to meet their Lord in the air,"§ and the waves of the great tribulation will have reached their highest tidal mark. But the infinite sign of life, "Sign of the Son of Man"¶ is seen in heaven, and with ten thousands of his saints, the judge of all the earth appears. The shuddering earth shrinks

* Isaiah liii. 7. ‡ Revelation xx. 1.
† I. John iii. 8. § I. Thessalonians iv. 17.
¶ See "Alpha and Omega."

destroy Evil? If so— Hell is terminated.
Rev 20:14-15

before the frown of the unveiled glorified One, and the **last supreme work** and sin **of** the great archangel, **with** his fallen prophet, goes down like Korah, Dathan, and Abiram, "quick into the pit."*

And the last enemy is put under his feet forever.† But through the balmy air of the purified creation, echoing from the jasper walls of the "city that hath foundations,"‡ swell out the wondrous strains of

THE WEDDING MARCH OF THE KING.

Saints, arise! in grace abounding;
Hark! the wedding march is sounding;
Read the times, with quick discerning;
See the signs of Christ's returning.

In the **sky** His flaming banner;
Lift your heads and shout, hosannah!
Trump of God the tidings summeth;
Saints, behold! the Bridegroom cometh!

Trumpets sounding, seven thunders,
Op'ning heavens, crowning wonders,
Usher in the consummation,
Mystery merged in revelation.

* Numbers xvi. **33.**   † Hebrews ii. **8.**   ‡ Hebrews xi. 10.

> Marching legions, heavens tremble,
> Soldiers of the cross assemble!
> Lightnings signal, thunders drumming,
> Wheel in line, The King is coming.

The portals swing wide before the countless hosts, and through the lifted gates the "ransomed of the Lord come to Zion with songs and everlasting joy upon their heads, while sorrow and sighing flee away"* forevermore. The heavenly choirs take up the mighty chorus, saying, "Alleluia; for the Lord God omnipotent reigneth. Let us be glad and rejoice, and give honor to him; for the marriage of the Lamb has come, and his wife hath made herself ready." †

The triumphant hosts sweep into the palace of the king, and there, the marriage spoiled on the site of Jerusalem of old, is restored in Jerusalem the new, and more than restored, for "Thy Maker is thy Husband," ‡ Baali gives place to Ishi,§ and his people are one in him, even as he is in the Father. There is room for all, and to

---

* Isaiah xxxv. 10.   † Revelation xix. 7.   ‡ Isaiah liv. 5.
§ Hosea ii. 16, 17; married to the Lord, not to the "lords" of the Baal worship.

Plate 41. THE HALLELUJAH CHORUS.

spare; and with the saints of all ages, the prophets and the patriarchs, the good and the great, the martyrs and the nobility of the suffering years, the overcomers of the serpent, who conquered through "the blood and the word of their testimony,"* sit down with their Lord in the "banqueting hall;" and "his banner over them is love."†

If there be anything in this little book that has caused a shudder; if there be anything apparently too offensive to be borne; if there be revealed any depth almost too profound for human credence; if there be any shadow seemingly cast upon cherished objects of faith and reverence; open your eyes to apprehend that the strength of the pain speaks the more of the power of the Healer, the sting of the offense testifies to the grace of the Burden-Bearer; the abysmal depth echoes with the name of Him who stooped down even there to save; and the shadows on the type but serve to bring out in startling relief the blazing light that streams about the Antitype.

* Revelation xii. 11. † Canticles ii. 4.

> Greater the foe, and stronger the fight,
> Greater the Victor; darker the night,
> Clearer the stars, in their heaven-born light,
> "Kept."
>
> Tell of the strength of the chains, now riven,
> Sweeter the tribute when "much forgiven,"
> Chief of the praises that ring in heaven,
> "Kept."

Scripture certainly does say these things. If they are not true the Bible is not true. But the voice of science loudly calls attention to the many strange facts and mysterious occurrences described in this book, and logically compares modern facts with ancient history, and equally ancient predictions concerning the last Age. The intelligent student who is capable of receiving evidence is forced to credit at least enough to convince him that all these things have begun to come to pass, and is ready to believe that this Age is drawing to a close, whatever may be the nature of the next; while the earnest believer in Revelation, with quickened pulse, and the joy of the great Hope thrilling every fibre of his being, hears anew the words of the Master, "Look up, and lift up your heads, for your redemption draweth nigh."

(The majority of men are incapable as jurors.) They cannot impartially weigh evidence, for with them some emotion, or sympathy, or prejudice overrides logic and calm judgment. Those, however, who can decide dispassionately often possess the elements necessary to leadership, and hence as they read and study over the facts presented in this book, conviction may follow judgment, and other voices be lifted against the partaking at the present time of the

TREE OF KNOWLEDGE.

www.ingramcontent.com/pod-product-compliance
Lightning Source LLC
Chambersburg PA
CBHW030549300426
44111CB00009B/920